Higher Text Plus

with Higher Fonts

by

Ron Aldrich
&
Darrell Aldrich

Produced by:
Brian Wiser & Bill Martens

 Apple PugetSound Program Library Exchange

Higher Text Plus

ISBN: 978-1-71672-724-5   2nd Edition

ACKNOWLEDGEMENTS

Our thanks to Robert C. Clardy, A.P.P.L.E. member and owner of Synergistic Software for continued permission to publish this software.

Higher Text II originally published by Synergistic Software in 1980.
Higher Text Plus originally published by A.P.P.L.E. in 1981.
Higher Text program copyright 1980 by Ron Aldrich and Darrell Aldrich.

Font Album (20 large and 24 small fonts) copyright 1984 by Wickerware Software.

Apple with TV art from *Higher Text II* manual originally designed by Anson.
Colorized and modified by Brian Wiser.

The Cover and Book were designed by Brian Wiser.

PRODUCTION

Brian Wiser   → Cover, Design, Layout, Editing
Bill Martens   → Additional Programming, Disk Updates
Antoine Vignau → Programming ProDOS version

DISCLAIMER

About the Authors

The Aldrich brothers, Ron and Darrell, were very prolific Apple II programmers who provided software in the early days to Synergistic Software and in turn to A.P.P.L.E. via Robert C. Clardy.

Together, they wrote a number of titles including several in the Academic Hallmarks produced Knowledge Master series in the areas of biology and earth sciences.

They also hold a number of patents in the area of glass coatings for insulation and have been prolific producers in the scientific community for many years

Ron and Darrell were single-handedly responsible for changing the way users presented text on a display when they wrote their best-selling *Higher Text* for the Apple II and the accompanying fonts – allowing users to present software that was not only impressive to see but also easy to use.

They both continue to reside in the Seattle, Washington area today.

About the Producers

Brian Wiser

Brian Wiser is a long-time consultant, enthusiast and historian of Apple, the Apple II and Macintosh. Steve Wozniak and Steve Jobs, as well as *Creative Computing, Nibble, InCider,* and *A+* magazines were early influences.

Brian designed, edited, and co-produced many books including: *Nibble Viewpoints: Business Insights From The Computing Revolution, Cyber Jack: The Adventures of Robert Clardy and Synergistic Software, Synergistic Software: The Early Games, The Colossal Computer Cartoon Book: Enhanced Edition, What's Where in the Apple: Enhanced Edition, Graphically Speaking: Enhanced Edition,* and *The WOZPAK: Special Edition* – an important Apple II historical book with Steve Wozniak's restored original, technical handwritten notes.

He passionately preserves and archives all facets of Apple's history, and noteworthy related companies such as Beagle Bros and Applied Engineering, featured on AppleArchives.com. His writing, interviews and books are featured on the technology news site CallApple.org and in *Call-A.P.P.L.E.* magazine that he co-produces. Brian also co-produced the retro iOS game *Structris.*

In 2005, Brian was cast as an extra in Joss Whedon's movie *Serenity,* leading him to being a producer and director for the documentary film *Done The Impossible: The Fans' Tale of Firefly & Serenity.* He brought some of the *Firefly* cast aboard his Browncoat Cruise and recruited several of the *Firefly* cast to appear in a film for charity. Brian speaks about his adventures to large audiences at conventions around the country.

Bill Martens

Bill Martens is a systems engineer specializing in office infrastructures and has been programming since 1976. The DEC PDP 11/40 with ASR-33 Teletypes and CRT's were his first computing platforms with his first forays in the Apple world coming with the Apple II computer.

Influences in Bill's computing life came from *Byte* magazine, *Creative Computing* magazine, and *Call-A.P.P.L.E.* magazine as well as his mentors Samuel Perkins, Don Williams, Joff Morgan, and Mike Christensen.

Bill is a co-producer of many books including *What's Where in the Apple: Enhanced Edition, The WOZPAK: Special Edition, Nibble Viewpoints: Business Insights From The Computing Revolution,* author of *Appilot/W1,* and co-programmer for the iOS version of the retro game *Structris.* He has written many articles which have appeared in user group newsletters and magazines such as *Call-A.P.P.L.E..*

Bill worked for Apple Pugetsound Program Library Exchange (A.P.P.L.E.) under Val Golding and Dick Hubert as a data manager and programmer in the 1980s, and is the current president of the A.P.P.L.E. user group established in 1978. He reorganized A.P.P.L.E. and restarted *Call-A.P.P.L.E.* magazine in 2002. He is the production editor for the A.P.P.L.E. website CallApple.org, writes science fiction novels in his spare time, and is a retired semi-pro football player.

I – Quick Reference Command Summaries

A. Generator Commands 1

B. Character Editor Commands 2

II – Overview

So now that I've got it, what do I do? 5

What's this about more than six hi-res colors? 6

Pretty Printing 7

Identical Editors are Like Identical Twins 7

Up, Up and Away (*Higher Text* in Action) 8

III – The Text Generator

Introduction 11

A. CHARACTER PARAMETERS 12

1. Font Sizes and Display Modes 13
   a. Large Font 13
   b. Medium Font 13
   c. Small Font Display Modes 13

2. Character Colors 14

3. Background Colors 16

4. Upper and Lower Case 17

B. CURSOR CONTROLS 18

C. SCREEN FUNCTIONS 18

1. Clearing Functions 18

2. Scrolling Functions 19

3. TEXT Command 19

IV – The Character Editors

Introduction 21

A. EDIT SYSTEM FEATURES 24

1. Entering and Exiting the Editors.................... 24

2. Loading and Saving Fonts and Generators............ 24

3. Moving Characters To and From the Edit Window....... 27

4. Swapping Large Font Characters 27

B. CHARACTER EDITING FEATURES 28

1. Clearing the Edit Window 28

2. Setting and Clearing Dots in the Matrix 28

3. Using the Edit Cursor 28

4. Scrolling a Character in the Edit Window........... 29

5. Inserting and Deleting Lines........................ 29

V – Technical Data

A. MEMORY ALLOCATION 31
1. Memory Map 31
2. Memory Usage by Higher Text and Friends 31
3. High Resolution Screen Pointers 33

B. FONT CONFIGURATIONS 34
1. Normal Configurations 34
2. Non-Standard Configurations 34
3. Calculating Font Indexes 35
4. Garbage Fonts 36

C. INTEGER BASIC HI-RES ROUTINES 36

D. CTRL-B[ackground] SCREEN FUNCTIONS 38

VI – General Information

A. CREATING YOUR OWN PROGRAM DISKETTE 43

B. SUBSIDIARY FUNCTIONS 44
1. Key Click 44
2. Control-G (bell) 44

C. SUPPORTING PROGRAMS 45
1. Program Line Editor 45
2. LOMEM: (The &LOMEM: Utility) 45
3. Billboard 46
   a. Slide Maker 46
   b. Climber 47
4. Higher Fonts & Font Previews 48
   a. Small Fonts (.SF) 49
   b. Medium Fonts (.MF) 61
   c. Large Fonts (.LF) 65
5. Demo Programs 87

VII – Glossary
.... 93

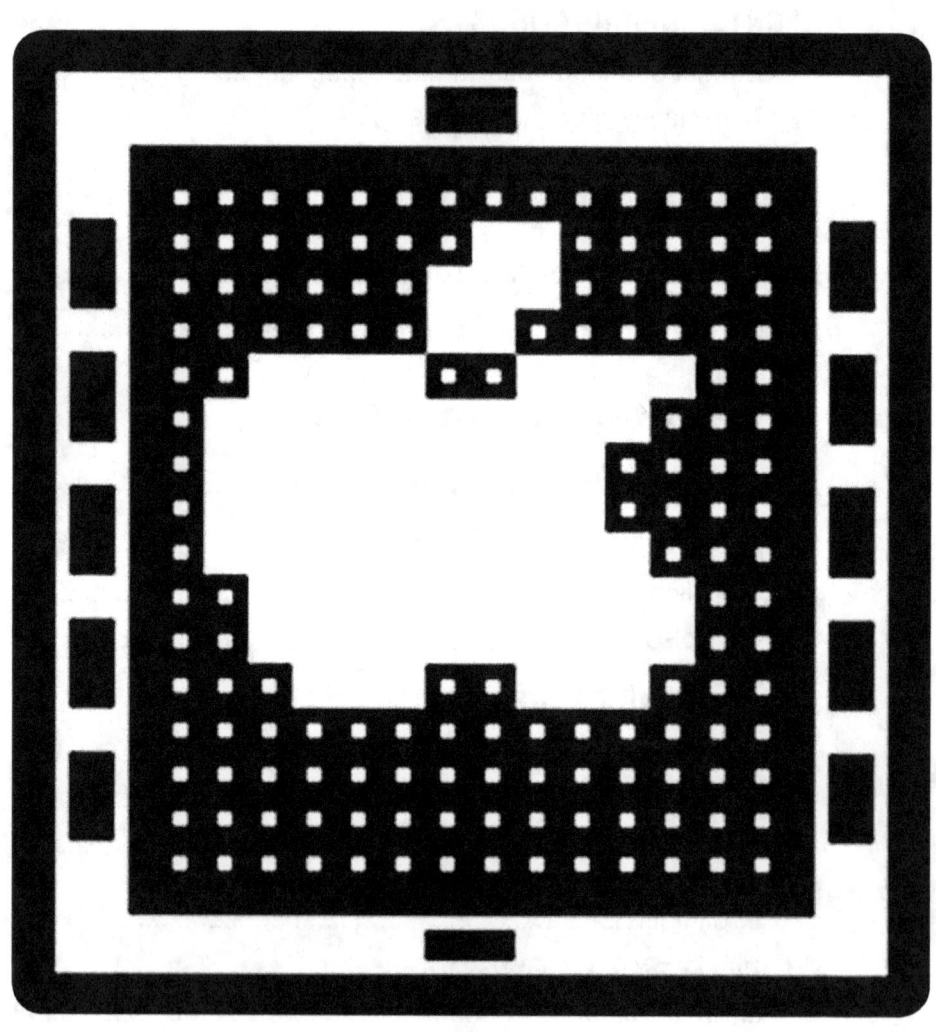

QUICK REFERENCE COMMAND SUMMARY

Generator Commands

Command	CHR$	Description	Page
CALL 3072	-	Cold start if HT generator in memory	9
CALL 3075	-	Warm start if HT generator in memory	9
CALL 3078	-	Turn off HT if HT generator in memory	10
Ctrl-Q	17	Select Large Font	13
Ctrl-E	5	Select Expanded Small Font display mode	14
Ctrl-R	18	Select Regular Small Font display mode	14
Ctrl-T	20	Select Tall Small Font display mode	14
Ctrl-W	23	Select Wide Small Font display mode	14
Ctrl-Y	25	Select Bold Face mode	14
Ctrl-Z	26	Deselect Bold Face mode	14
Ctrl-C+	3+	Color assignment prefix	15
Ctrl-B0	2+0	Assign Current Color to Background	16
Ctrl-A*	-	Upper Case shift lock	17
Ctrl-S*	-	Lower Case shift lock	17
Ctrl-X*	-	Cancel current line being typed	17
Ctrl-H	-	Move cursor one position Left	18
Ctrl-I	-	Move cursor one position Right	18
Ctrl-J	-	Move cursor one line Down	18
Ctrl-K	-	Move cursor one line Up	18
Ctrl-L	12	Clear screen, Home cursor	18
Ctrl-N	14	Clear from cursor to end of Current Line	18
Ctrl-O	15	Clear from cursor to end of Page	18
Ctrl-F	6	Scroll text Up one line	19
Ctrl-P	16	Select Smooth scroll mode	19
Ctrl-@	0	Deselect Smooth scroll mode	19
Ctrl-B+	2+	Background mode assignment prefix	38
Ctrl-V*	-	Select or Deselect Key Click function	44
Ctrl-G	7	Bell	44

* May be used in immediate mode (from keyboard) only
+ Indicates suffix required

1

Character Editor Commands

SYSTEM COMMANDS

Command	Description	Page
Ctrl-L[ower]	Select/deselect Large Font lower case	23
1	Select Small Font 1	23
2	Select Small Font 2	23
3	Select Small Font 3	23
Ctrl-C[ancel]	Exit editor, return to BASIC	24
RUN	Return to editor from BASIC	24
E[ditor]	Run the editor not currently in use	24
D[isk]	Display disk catalog	26
L[oad]	Load a font from disk	26
O[utput]	Output (save) a font to disk	25
I	Move system cursor up one line	27
J	Move system cursor left one position	27
K	Move system cursor right one position	27
L	Move system cursor down one line	27
P[lace]	Place a character in the edit window	27
[Return]	Return a character from edit window to font	28
R[estart]	Clear edit window, restart editing	28
X	Set a dot in matrix (X marks the spot)	28
C[lear]	Clear a dot in the matrix	28

EDIT WINDOW COMMANDS

Command	Description	Page
W	Move edit cursor Up one line	28
A	Move edit cursor Left one position	28
S	Move edit cursor Right one position	28
Z	Move edit cursor Down one line	28
Ctrl-W	Scroll character in edit window Up 1 line	28
Ctrl-A	Scroll character in edit window Left 1 position	28
Ctrl-S	Scroll character in edit window Right 1 position	28
Ctrl-Z	Scroll character in edit window Down 1 line	28
Y	Delete Horizontal line at edit cursor position	29
G	Delete Vertical line at edit cursor position	29
H	Insert Vertical line at edit cursor position	29
B	Insert Horizontal line at edit cursor position	29

GAMES

DEMOS

EDUCATIONAL PROGRAMS

MUCH, MUCH MORE...

FOR INSTANCE... MATH

$$\sum_{i=1}^{n} a_i + \sum_{i=1}^{n} b_i = (a_1 + a_2 + \cdots + a_n) + (b_1 + b_2 + \cdots + b_n)$$

$$= (a_1 + b_1) + (a_2 + b_2) + \cdots + (a_n + b_n)$$

$$= \sum_{i=1}^{n} (a_1 + b_1)$$

Seven different
character types

REGULAR

TALL

BOLDFACE

WIDE

EXPANDED

LARGE FONT

OVERVIEW

Higher Text Plus is a complete package for producing text on either high-resolution graphic screen. The *Higher Text* diskette, available at www.callapple.org, includes 93 complete upper and lower case 96 character ASCII character sets. Examples of the included fonts may be found in Section VI. Characters may be printed in several sizes, shapes and colors, with selectable background colors and modes. Two editors are provided for modifying any individual character, or designing your own entire character set. Higher Text allows you to print on the hi-res screens with PRINT, VTAB and HTAB [TAB] statements, exactly as if you were printing to the regular text screen.

So now that I've got it, what can it do?

It would almost be simpler to list what *Higher Text* cannot do. *Higher Text* is without question, the finest program of its kind written for the Apple II. *Higher Text* comes with 93 character sets, also known as "fonts," identified on the catalog by the suffix ".SF" (Small fonts), ".MF" (Medium fonts), and ".LF" (Large fonts). In addition, separate diskettes are available that contain many more fonts, thus it is possible to use any one or more of these fonts in your Applesoft or Integer BASIC hi-res program, without needing to create your own.

In this introductory section, we will describe briefly some of the characteristics of *Higher Text* and their respective applications. *Higher Text* is a complex system which effectively converts your hi-res screen to function as a regular text screen, but with the added facilities of up to ten colors and multiple character sizes. It is composed of two main bodies, the character generator and the character editor.

The character generator is that part of the *Higher Text* System which interprets the BASIC program lines, converts them to instructions understandable by the Apple II hi-res graphics routines, places the specified characters at the desired locations on the hi-res screen, and contains within it one complete small font and an upper case large font.

The character editor is that part of *Higher Text* which you control to modify or redefine characters. Two cursor oriented editors make up this one module. The capability to create your own fonts, or to modify existing ones, is handled by these editors, one for small fonts, and one for large fonts.

Character sets you have developed or modified may be saved in two different ways:

1. As a font which can be loaded back into *Higher Text* at any time, or

2. As a generator, which can be saved on a separate diskette, along with your BASIC program.

What's this about more than six Hi-Res colors?

There is a technique known as "dithering" which is very much like mixing two colors of paint together to produce another color. As in paint, when blue and yellow are mixed to produce green, the original pigments remain, and it is the illusion of seeing these bits of pigments so close together that we accept as a new color. So it is in hi-res graphics when adjacent dots on the screen are "mixed." It appears to our eyes that we have created a new color. Just as when you mix a gallon of blue paint and a gallon of yellow, you end up with two gallons of green. When you "mix" two vertical dot rows in hi-res, you end up with twice the number of dots, thus the four additional colors of yellow, lavender, pink and aqua are available in the "expanded" character mode only.

Pretty Printing

Large fonts (.LF) are composed from a 14x16 dot matrix and have but one display mode. They may be displayed in any of the six BASIC hi-res colors.

Small fonts (.SF) are developed from a 7x8 dot matrix, and may be displayed in any of the available display modes, Regular, Wide, Tall, and Expanded, and in up to six hi-res colors, plus four additional colors that may be used with the Expanded mode only.

The Wide and Expanded modes may be displayed on a background of any of the six standard hi-res colors, and a table has been provided to explain how text/background mixtures are obtained. As a consequence of limitations inherent in the Apple II hi-res display, results may not be as you anticipate, thus selection of text and background colors must be undertaken with care. For example, to print orange text on a white background, blue must be selected as the text color. Except when a black background has been chosen, the text color displayed will be the complement of the text color selected.

Identical Editors are Like Identical Twins

As indicated previously, two editors are supplied, one for the small font group and one for a large font. Each performs its chores in an identical manner. Two cursors are provided. One is used to select the character you wish to edit, and the second cursor is the edit cursor which is used in the edit window to set or clear points in the matrix.

Several options and combinations are available for saving an entire font or generator to disk. When using the small font editor, three complete fonts, numbered 1, 2, and 3, are always displayed on the screen. Any one font may be saved individually, or all three may be saved at the same time. In addition, you may save a large font without a lower case and one small font together. All possible combinations of saving various fonts and generators together are described in detail in the section on the character editor.

Up, Up and Away (*Higher Text* in Action)

Throughout this manual, wherever there are procedural differences between Applesoft BASIC and Integer BASIC, the Integer BASIC function will be shown second, enclosed in square brackets. In program listings, those pertaining only to Applesoft will be preceded by a right square bracket (]); those pertaining only to Integer will be preceded by a right angle bracket (>). If a program line is bilingual (so to speak), no special notation will be used.

Similarly, references to hexadecimal addresses throughout will be preceded by a dollar sign ($), and followed by a decimal address enclosed in square brackets.

When you boot on the *Higher Text* diskette, it will automatically configure itself to your system. If you have an Apple II Plus, the BASIC programs will be in Applesoft. If for any reason you wish to reconfigure your *Higher Text* diskette, enter either FP or INT from the keyboard, whichever is appropriate, and BRUN BOOT. The disk must not be write protected when BRUNing BOOT.

After BRUNing Higher Text, or following a boot, a four choice menu will appear. Selection one is entitled DEMO, which we suggest you try before reading further in this manual. DEMO will show you in a moment or two, the very sophisticated uses to which *Higher Text* may be put. In addition, if you have Integer BASIC available, you may run from the keyboard the program DEMO 48, which is an expanded version of the DEMO program on the menu.

If you exit the menu with choice four, EXIT, you will return to command mode, but with a difference. *Higher Text* will still be up and running, and you will still be viewing the hi-res screen. Each of the character generator command codes will perform their expected functions, and you may enjoy the novelty of looking at your catalog displayed in any font mode. Just enter a Ctrl-Q for the large font, carriage return and then type catalog as you normally would. Note that if you are in lower case mode, neither DOS nor BASIC will recognize any commands you may type.

Should you list a program while *Higher Text* is up, any control characters imbedded in the listing will be implemented by *Higher Text*, thus you may see your list change fonts and/or colors from line to line, etc. It is probably a good idea to exit Higher Text with RESET if you are seriously interested in examining the listing. *Higher Text* may be reentered with a CALL 3075 which will preserve all variables and data, or a CALL 3072 for a "cold" start. If you inadvertently exit either editor with a Ctrl-C, you may return to the editor and save all data with a RUN.

To actually use one of the *Higher Text* fonts in your own program, the font must first be saved as a generator, not a font, using a file name of your choice. Then you must enter the following two lines in an Applesoft program; line 20 only for an Integer program.

```
  10 PRINT CHR$(4) "BRUN LOMEM :": &LOMEM: 16384
  20 PRINT CHR$(4) "BRUN FILENAME"
> 20 PRINT D$; "BRUN FILENAME": REM D$ = Ctrl D
```

Applesoft requires that the start of program be moved upward in memory, which is accomplished by the &LOMEM: program. If you wish to use hi-res screen two, the 16384 should be replaced with

24576. Filename is, of course, the name under which you have saved your generator. Line 10 is not required by Integer BASIC. Lines 10 and 20 should be entered prior to declaring any variables.

Preceding this section are two summaries of *Higher Text* commands, one each for the generator and the editor. Each summary is indexed with a page number where special information on the referenced command may be found.

Special note should be taken that the commands for the generator are all control characters, while those for the editor are regular characters, except where specifically shown as "ctrl [chr]". A control character is entered by holding the control key down, while at the same time depressing the character key specified.

Sections III and IV are devoted to functional descriptions and examples of each feature of the generator and editor, respectively. Section V is for the brave of heart who are interested in knowing details that have been omitted from Sections III and IV, including a memory map and important addresses.

Section VI describes use of the &LOMEM: utility and the Improved Integer BASIC Hi-res [*WOZPAK*] routines, and Section VII is a glossary of terms used in this manual.

For the ProDOS 8 version of *Higher Text Plus*, the &LOMEM utility is not used. BLOAD HIGHER.TEXT will load the HT generator at $0C00. Then, load your Applesoft program in either part of the Apple II memory – this example will execute the Applesoft program at $6001:

```
POKE 103,1:POKE 104,96:POKE 24576,0:RUN PROGRAM
```

A new entry point was added for the ProDOS 8 version of *Higher Text Plus*. CALL 3078 will deactivate the HT generator is already memory. Used in conjunction with TEXT and HOME, it allows you to switch back to the standard text interface of your Apple II. CALL 3072 or CALL 3075 will activate the HT generator again.

THE TEXT GENERATOR

The text generator is the program on the *Higher Text* diskette that is named "Higher Text". It contains within it $C00 [3072] bytes of character fonts. You may, if desired, load a font from the disk by its file name, or use the font that *Higher Text* automatically loads in when it is run or booted. Additional fonts may be saved in various portions of free memory as indicated herein. Figure 2 on page 25, shows the three possible configurations of fonts within a generator. A generator is SAVEd from either of the two editors, using a file name of your choice, and it is this generator that enables your BASIC program to make use of the *Higher Text* fonts.

As explained on page 25, the usual method of using *Higher Text*, or a Higher Text generator from your BASIC program, is with the BRUN command. However, there may be occasions when you do not wish the generator to be brought up immediately, in which case the generator may be BLOADed, and later activated with a CALL 3072. Note this does not eliminate the need in Applesoft to BRUN and use the &LOMEM: 16384 (or 24576) prior to declaring any variables. Further information on & LOMEM : may be found in Section VI.

If *Higher Text* or a generator has already been BRUN and you wish to disable it for any reason, this may be done with a PRINT CHR$(4) [Ctrl-D] ; "PR#0": PRINT CHR$(4) [Ctrl-D] ; "IN#0". The PRINT CHR$(4) [Ctrl-D] is not required from immediate mode. A

CALL 3075 will restart *Higher Text* with all fonts and variables intact. This is called the "warm start" address because it preserves all data. The "cold start" address is CALL 3072, which would destroy all variables and start from scratch. These are covered in this section:

    A. Character Parameters
        1. Font Sizes and Display Modes
        2. Character Colors
        3. Background Colors
        4. Upper and Lower Case
    B. Cursor Controls
    C. Screen Functions

All control functions in the generator, with the exception of upper and lower case shift locks, are fully programmable, meaning they may be imbedded in your BASIC program lines. You may find it convenient in Applesoft to substitute the equivalent CHR$(n) for the control character you wish to use. If control functions are entered as separate PRINT statements, then they should be followed with a semicolon (;) to avoid unintentional scrolling.

A. Character Parameters

Text characters can be operated upon in five different ways:

    – You may choose the font size (large or small)
    – You may choose the display mode of a small font
    – You may choose the font color
    – You may choose the background color in some cases
    – You may choose upper or lower case.

Any of the above characteristics may be intermixed within a single PRINT statement, provided that the display parameters and requirements for the specific selection are adhered to. For example, if you have selected a pink expanded character, you cannot change to a tall character, because a tall character will not display in pink. Text is entered normally, exactly as you would do when writing a PRINT, INPUT or REM statement to the regular text screen. All the usual commands are recognized : HOME [CALL -936], TEXT, HTAB [TAB], VTAB, etc. (See TEXT command on page 19.)

Your best guide in learning to correctly select the character specifications you desire, is by first entering and observing the results of the short sample programs at the conclusion of this manual, and then, using those programs as examples, write your own test programs. These will determine if the control characters you have entered indeed produce the desired effect. In addition, the DEMO program in Section V. (D) may be of help.

1. Font Sizes and Display Modes

a. Large Font

The large font will display 12 lines of 20 characters, and is selected preceding a PRINT statement with CHR$(17) [Ctrl-Q]. It may be displayed in standard colors on colored backgrounds.

b. Medium Font

Medium fonts use the Large Fonts editor but only use a portion of the area. While large fonts use seven lines of the grid for the full set, medium fonts only use five. Also, most medium fonts are only 10 x 12 dots to 12 x 12 dots. There are a few exceptions which are 13 x 12, but the height is always 12.

c. Small Font Display Modes

There are four small font display modes: Regular, Wide, Tall and Expanded. They are all formed from a 7x8 dot matrix and are identified by their screen format characteristics, which are set forth in Table I. In addition, each of the four display modes has its own intrinsic features, also detailed in Table I, along with the appropriate commands to select each mode.

The Wide and Expanded characters are the only ones that may be displayed against a colored background. Table II lists the necessary text and background color selections to achieve the desired color mix for the Wide or Expanded display mode. Regular and Tall characters have a secondary display mode referred to as bold face. This is similar to the bold face or enhanced mode of some hard copy printers, where the method used is to overstrike the characters at a one dot offset. Bold face mode is selected with CHR$(25) [Ctrl-Y] and deselected with CHR$(26) [Ctrl-Z].

2. Character Colors

The assignment of character colors in *Higher Text* appears at first to be a rather complex proceeding, because of the variety of combinations of font sizes, classes, colors, and background colors. That each class may not be displayed in each available mode or color is again a result of the limitations of the Apple high resolution video display. After some experimentation, it will be found to be simpler than it appears.

The next paragraphs attempt to define the color choice selections available to each of the font characters, and how to enable them. You are additionally referred to the program examples given later in this document. Three font display modes will display characters in six colors: Expanded, Wide, and Large. Also, the Expanded mode may be displayed in four "dithered" colors: yellow, lavender, pink, and aqua.

TABLE I
Font Display Modes

Character Display Mode	Matrix Size	Screen Format, Lines of Chrs.		Select Display Mode with: Ctrl CHR$		Select Bold Face with: Ctrl CHR$		Deselect Bold Face with: Ctrl CHR$		Bkgnd Colors Avail	Character Colors Avail *
Large	14x16	12	20	Q	17					6	6
Regular	7x8	24	40	R	18	Y	25	Z	26	2	2
Tall	7x8	12	40	T	20	Y	25	Z	26	2	2
Wide	7x8	24	20	W	23					6	6
Expanded	7x8	12	20	E	5					6	10

* In some cases, additional character colors may be used, but some characters will be imperfect, depending on where they are placed on the screen, and the background color present.

Table II is a chart which contains the various character and background color command codes, and the resulting combinations of text and background colors produced by each. In some cases, more than one set of command codes will produce the same combination of text and background color. These are marked as "alternate" and set in italic type. Other command code combinations not listed in the table produce undesirable results, such as a colored character on a horizontally striped two color background. In certain cases these combinations may be used for special effects, which can be found through experimentation, then recorded for future use.

TABLE II

Background/Character Color Selection Chart

			CHARACTER COLOR SELECTION								
CHR Color ▶ PRINT ▶			White Ctrl C0	Green Ctrl C1	Violet Ctrl C2	Orange Ctrl C3	Blue Ctrl C4	Yellow Ctrl C5	Lavender Ctrl C6	Pink Ctrl C7	Aqua Ctrl C8
DSP MODE ▶			EWL RT	E W L	E W L	E W L	E W L	E	E	E	E
BACKGROUND COLOR SELECTION	WHITE Ctrl C0 Ctrl B0	T X T / B G	Black / White	Violet / White	Green / White	Aqua / White	Orange / White	Blue / White	Grn/Orng. / White	Grn./Blk. / White	Pink/Blk. / White
	GREEN Ctrl C1 Ctrl B0	T X T / B G	– / –	Black / Green	White / Green	alt. Black / Orange	alt. White / Orange	– / –	– / –	– / –	– / –
	VIOLET Ctrl C2 Ctrl B0	T X T / B G	– / –	White / Violet	Black / Violet	alt. White / Blue	alt. Black / Blue	– / –	– / –	– / –	– / –
	ORANGE Ctrl C3 Ctrl B0	T X T / B G	– / –	alt. Black / Green	alt. White / Green	Black / Orange	White / Orange	– / –	– / –	– / –	– / –
	BLUE Ctrl C4 Ctrl B0	T X T / B G	– / –	alt. White / Violet	alt. Black / Violet	White / Blue	Black / Blue	– / –	– / –	– / –	– / –
	BLACK Ctrl C9 Ctrl B0	T X T / B G	White / Black	Green / Black	Violet / Black	Orange / Black	Blue / Black	Yellow / Black	Lavender / Black	Pink / Black	Aqua / Black

Selection of BLACK [Ctrl C9] as a Character Color will result in a character the same color as the background useful only as XDRAW.

3. Background Colors

All characters may be displayed against black or white backgrounds. The Expanded, Wide or Large modes may in addition be displayed against the other four available colored backgrounds. Setting a colored background is a wee bit tricky, since two command functions are required, and except on black backgrounds, the text color selected will produce its complement. The available combinations are shown in Table II.

The background color subroutine uses the text color command code as the first of two steps, thus text color selection must be made after establishing the background color.

After deciding upon the combination of text and background colors you wish to use, first choose a background color by PRINTing Ctrl Cn, where n=a color from 0 to 4, or 9, from the color command code list, then PRINT a Ctrl B0 to pass the chosen color on to *Higher Text's* background color subroutine. For example, to print Expanded orange characters on a white background:

```
] 100    PRINT CHR$(5);
> 100    PRINT"";: REM CTRL-E IN QUOTES
  101    REM SELECT EXPANDED CHR MODE
  110    PRINT "0": REM SELECT WHITE BG
  111    REM CTRL-C PRECEDES 0 IN QUOTES
  112    REM 0 WILL NOT LIST IF HIGHER TEXT IS UP
  120    PRINT "0";: REM PASS INFO TO BG ROUTINE
  121    REM CTRL-B PRECEDES 0 IN QUOTES
  122    REM SEE 112
  130    PRINT "4";: REM SELECT BLUE TO PRODUCE ORANGE CHR
  131    REM CTRL-C PRECEDES 4 IN QUOTES
  132    REM SEE 112
  140    PRINT "HELLO": END
```

This procedure can be simplified considerably by concatenating the required characters into an Applesoft string or, in either language, entering the characters directly into a string, as shown in the following examples:

```
150  SETUP$=CHR$(4)+"0"+CHR$(3)+"0"+CHR$(4)+"4":
     REM SET EXP.WHITE BG, ORANGE CHRS
160  PRINT SETUP$; "HELLO": END or
170  DIM SETUP$(10): SETUP$="c0b0c4" REM small
     chars represent ctrl chars
180  PRINT SETUP$; "HELLO: END
```

There are a few rare situations for example where you might wish to place *Higher Text* characters on an existing screen that shows a graph, etc. in which the *Higher Text* background conflicts with that of the graph. In this event, *Higher Text* has provided several alternatives through the Ctrl-L (Background) function. Details on these alternate background display modes may be found in the technical section, Part D.

4. Upper and Lower Case

Higher Text has provided a simple means for the direct entry of lower case characters through the use of two shift lock functions: Control-A, upper case shift lock, and Control-S, lower case shift lock. These two control characters will not be entered into the text, as they are used in the immediate mode only. Once lower case characters have been entered, they remain a part of the program, regardless of whether or not Higher Text is "up" or in use.

After typing a Ctrl-S, all following characters will be in lower case until one of the following conditions is met:

- A Ctrl-A is entered (the following characters will revert to upper case)
- A carriage return is entered (the program line as it exists will be entered into memory)
- A Ctrl-X is entered (the current line will be cancelled as in the normal Ctrl-X function)

Following any of the above actions, the next characters typed will be in upper case. You are reminded that neither DOS nor BASIC will recognize commands or variable names typed in lower case, thus a Ctrl-A must always be typed in a program line just prior to a command, if your current mode is lower case. Lower case may be used in any PRINT, REM, or INPUT statements. Lower case characters may only be typed while *Higher Text*, *Program Line Editor* or similar entry methods are up.

B. Cursor Controls

Four limited use cursor commands are provided in the *Higher Text* generator. These have the effect of moving the cursor in a PRINT or REM statement in accordance with the control used. A Control-H and Control-I duplicate the functions of the left and right arrow keys, respectively, except the Control-H will not be entered into the line of text. A Control-J duplicates the function of Control-J in the Apple, i.e., a line feed. The Control-K is the most useful of the cursor functions in that it provides a reverse scroll, performing the inverse of a Control-J. Try this example to get the idea:

```
100   PRINT "HELLO kkk GOODBYE"
```

where the small "k" represents a Control-K. Try both listing and running the program and observe the interesting results.

C. Screen Functions

Two types of screen controls exist in *Higher Text*, those which clear the screen, and those which scroll the screen. There are three of each type, and each is enabled by the control characters shown in the following table. Reminder: type the control key and the alphabetic character key simultaneously, just as when using the shift key.

1. Clearing Functions

CHR$	CTRL	FUNCTION PERFORMED
12	L	Clears screen, Homes cursor
14	N	Clears current line from cursor position to end of line
15	O	Clears from cursor position to end of page

2. Scrolling Functions

CHR$	CTRL	FUNCTION PERFORMED
6	F	Scrolls text Up one line
16	P	Turns On smooth scroll mode
0	@	Turns Off smooth scroll mode.

Each of the preceding commands may be entered in program lines or used from immediate mode. In Integer BASIC, the control character must be placed in a PRINT statement or assigned to a string. Applesoft provides the additional capability of PRINTing the equivalent CHR$ function.

While *Higher Text* is up, if a program line is listed, you may notice a rather shaky scrolling motion as each line scrolls up. This is characteristic of a "normal" scroll on the high resolution screen. As shown in the table above, *Higher Text* also provides a super smooth scrolling feature. It is, however, considerably slower than the standard scroll, thus it is up to you to determine which method best suits your needs.

3. TEXT Command

The *Higher Text* TEXT command varies somewhat from the normal Apple usage, in that while it resets the scroll window, it does not return to the standard text mode, but remains on the current hi-res page. TEXT functions only in direct mode: under program control, a CALL -1220 should be used for the same function.

WELCOME TO
HIGHER TEXT

1. DEMO
2. LARGE FONT EDITOR
3. SMALL FONT EDITOR
4. EXIT

SELECT OPTION ▮

Introduction

The Character Editor is the portion of *Higher Text* where you create or modify characters. Actually there are two complete editors, one for the 14x16 matrix (large font) and one for the 7x8 matrix (small font). Each functions in an identical manner, and will be treated here as a single editor, except where differences exist.

The editor itself is divided into two modules. One module handles the system chores, such as selecting the character to be edited, moving it to and from the edit window, loading and saving fonts and generators, etc. The second module performs the actual editing, moving the character within the matrix, inserting and deleting lines, etc. Each module is equipped with its own cursor, referred to hereafter as the system cursor and the edit cursor, respectively.

In rather general terms, you may wish to load a font, select a character with the system cursor, move it into the edit window where it can be manipulated, change its appearance by editing with the various available commands, return it to the character set, and either save the font with the modified character or select a new character and repeat the procedure.

Figure 1A shows the actual screen display provided by the Large Font Editor. The lower portion of the screen displays the current large font, which occupies four lines of 16 characters each. Control-L is a toggle. If Control-L is pressed, two additional lines, representing the lower case characters, will appear on the screen. Pressing Control-L a second time will return the font to its previous state. Upon first entering the editor, the system cursor will be found in its home position, over the rightmost character of the last line. When Control-L is toggled, the system cursor will home to the new last line.

FIGURE 1A

Centered above the font is a 14x16 dot matrix. This is the edit window, and the edit cursor will be found in its home position, the upper left corner. Each editor is equipped with a view window to the right of the edit window. When a character has been placed in the edit window, the view window will display it, full size, in each of the six possible colors, just as it would appear in your program. It is important to check the view window while editing, as some combinations of adjacent dots may produce undesirable effects in certain colors.

Figure 1B shows the actual screen display provided by the Small Font Editor. Three small fonts are displayed together, in an L-shaped pattern, with the edit window to the right of the upper font (number 1), which is the default font. Small font number 2 is at the lower left, and number 3 is at the lower right. Entering a 1, 2, or 3 will select the corresponding small font, and the system cursor will be placed at its home position at the lower right corner of the selected font. Initially, if the system cursor has been moved from its home position, and a new font is selected with the 1, 2 or 3, then the system cursor will be placed over the same relative character as in the previous font. Each of the three small fonts are complete with both upper and lower case.

FIGURE 1B

The view window in the small font editor serves a purpose similar to that of the large font. It displays the current character being edited in each of the six possible display modes, i.e., regular, bold, tall, wide, narrow or expanded. Again, it is important to check each character being edited in the view window, as it is possible that some combinations of adjacent dots may produce undesirable effects in certain display modes.

A. Edit System Features

1. Entering and Exiting the Editors

Three avenues of entry for the edit module exist. You may:

1. Boot the disk, or
2. RUN Hello and select either editor from choices 2 and 3 on the menu, or
3. Type "RUN EDIT.SM (or) EDIT.LG" for the small font and large font editors, respectively, or if you have inadvertently left either editor and have not loaded another program, you may re-enter with a RUN, and all characters will be as you left them.

To exit either editor, you may type a Control-C, which will return you to immediate mode, with *Higher Text* still up, or you may type 'E' to select the other editor. If you type an E, you will be asked "RUN LARGE [SMALL) FONT EDITOR (Y/N) ". A 'N' response will give you the opportunity to back out, in the event you typed the E in error.

2. Loading & Saving Fonts & Generators

Let's get into this one by explaining again what a font is and what a generator is, and the various font/generator combinations. A *Higher Text* character font has three possible configurations, which are shown in Figure 2A. Generator is a font plus the *Higher Text* Operating System. In fact, the program named *Higher Text* is a generator, and is composed of nothing more than the *Higher Text* operating system and the default font that is supplied as an intrinsic part of the *Higher Text Plus* package.

A font or a generator may be saved from or loaded into the editor in accordance with the configurations shown in Figure 2. The criterion in determining whether you should save a font or a generator is its intended use. If it is one of a number of fonts you may wish to use at some time in the future, you probably would want to save it as a font only. If you are saving it to a separate diskette and have a specific application for it in a program, you should save it as a generator. To utilize a generator in your program, it must either be BRUN, or else BLOADed and enabled with a CALL 3072.

FIGURE 2

Higher Text Font Configurations

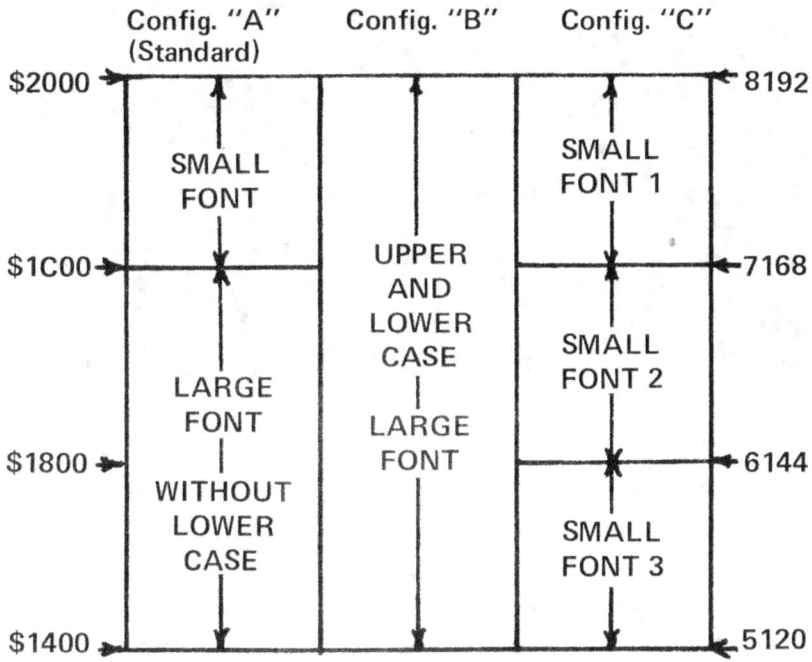

From within the editor, the O[utput] command is used to save either a font or generator to disk. When you type the 'O', the editor will ask whether you wish to save a font or a generator, and the appropriate answer should be made. Note that if you wish a suffix to be added to the filename of the font or generator, it must be specified at this time, as it is not done automatically.

The L[oad] command is used to load a font. Before you type the 'L', make certain you know the name of the font. The full name of the font should be specified, including any suffix. If you cannot remember the name of the font you want to load or save, type a 'D' (for Disk catalog) to refresh your memory. If you plunge madly ahead and attempt to load a non-existent file name, an error may result. However, entering a carriage return in response to the file name query will return you to the editor safe and sound, with no file loaded.

If you are using the small font editor when you go to load a file, you will be asked an additional question: "Normal Location (Y/1/2/3)". Normally, you would respond with a 'Y', which will load either a font or a generator. However, if you are loading a single small font, a numeric response may be used to "force" it into the specified location. The number selected would coincide with the fonts shown in Figure 1B.

3. Moving Characters To and From the Edit Window

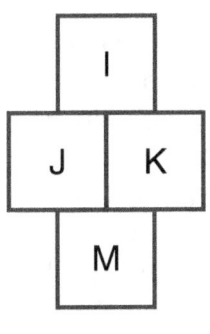

FIGURE 3

The system cursor is used to select the character from the displayed font that you wish to edit. Likewise, after editing a character, the position of the system cursor determines where that character will be returned to the displayed font. Four keys are used, 'I', 'J', 'K', and 'M', representing up, left, right, and down. You will note these keys are arranged in a cluster which simulates the points of a compass, as shown in Figure 3.

When the system cursor has been placed over the character selected for editing, a 'P' will P[lace] the character in the edit window, where any operation may be performed on it. After editing, a [RETURN] will return the character to the position in the font shown by the system cursor. If you wish to return the character elsewhere in the font, the system cursor must be moved to that position before hitting return.

4. Swapping Large Font Characters

A situation may arise where you need a single character from a font not currently in memory. This may be accomplished by BLOADing the alternate font. BSAVEing the desired character in accordance with the below formula, reBLOADing the original large font, BLOADing the single character (again from the formula below), and finally outputting the modified font to disk.

Take the ASCII value of the character to be swapped, subtract $20 [32], multiply the result by $20 [32], and add this to $1400 [5120]. This will be the A$ [A] parameter for the BSAVE/BLOAD, and $20 [32] will be the L$ [L] parameter.

B. Character Editing Features

1. Clearing the Edit Window

There are two ways to clear the edit window. When a character has been completed and [RETURN]ed to the font, the window will automatically be cleared. If you are creating a character from scratch (i.e., one that has not been P[lace] d in the edit window) and have made such a botch of it that you wish to start over, the R[estart] command will also clear the edit window. However, if you are working on a character from the font and wish to restart, you should just type a 'P' and the same character will be placed in the edit window again, exactly as it was when you commenced editing.

2. Setting & Clearing Dots in the Matrix

When the edit cursor is covering a dot that is to be added to the current character, enter 'X' to set the dot. (X marks the spot!) If you wish to remove a dot from the current character, typing a 'C' will clear it. The commands 'X' and 'C' may be typed at any time during editing.

3. Using the Edit Cursor

The position of the edit cursor determines where in the matrix a dot will be set or cleared. The edit cursor is configured exactly like the system cursor in that the function keys are arranged like the points of a compass. The edit cursor uses the commands 'W', 'A', 'S', and 'Z' to move the cursor up, left, right, and down, as shown in Figure 4.

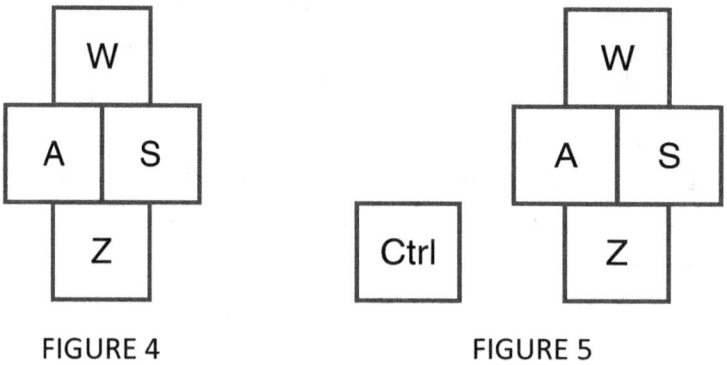

FIGURE 4   FIGURE 5

4. Scrolling a Character in Edit Window

There are times when you may wish to scroll the character in the edit window, for example in modifying an "A" to an "Æ", you might wish to move the original "A" one or two dot positions to the left. The four control characters shown in Figure 5, Ctrl-W, Ctrl-A, Ctrl-S, and Ctrl-Z will scroll the character up, left, right, or down. Note again the keypad/compass point arrangement. In our example above, if you wish to shift the "A" two dot positions left, you would hold the Ctrl key down and type AA.

5. Inserting and Deleting Lines

The insert/delete function has the effect of doing a partial scroll. If, for example, you wished to make a character taller, you no doubt would want to add dots at some appropriate place in the middle of the character. To do this, you would position the edit cursor at the location where you wanted to add a line, and type 'B', which would scroll that portion of the character at the cursor position downward, leaving a "blank" line where you could then set dots as needed. Conversely, a 'Y' would delete one horizontal line and shift the remainder of the character up one dot row.

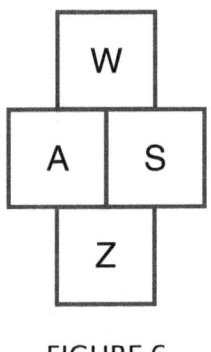

FIGURE 6

The Insert/Delete key cluster is shown in Figure 6, and the four compass commands are Y=delete horizontal line, G=delete vertical line, H=insert vertical line, and B=insert horizontal line.

A. Memory Allocation

1. Memory Map

Figure 7 on page 32 shows complete memory allocations for the Apple II, including areas used by *Higher Text* and *Program Line Editor*.

2. Memory Usage by Higher Text & Friends

The Higher Text generator resides from $C00 [3072] to $13FF [5119]. In addition, it makes liberal use of the Page 3 area from $300 [768] to $32F [815], for scratch storage and flags, etc., as detailed in Table III on page 33.

The &LOMEM: utility uses Page 3 from $330 [816] to $3CF [975]. However, once &LOMEM: has been called, and the new start of an Applesoft program set, then assuming there is no further requirement for this utility, the space may be used for user routines as needed. This area is available at any time from an Integer BASIC program. From $3D0 [976] to $3FF [1023] is used by DOS and monitor for various vectors, etc., and hence is unavailable.

The Integer BASIC High-Resolution graphics routines use the area from $7FD [2045] to $BFF [3071], and are used from both Integer BASIC and Applesoft programs. However, in Applesoft, if HGR or HGR2 is executed prior to BRUNning *Higher Text* or a generator, then this area becomes available for other use.

FIGURE 7

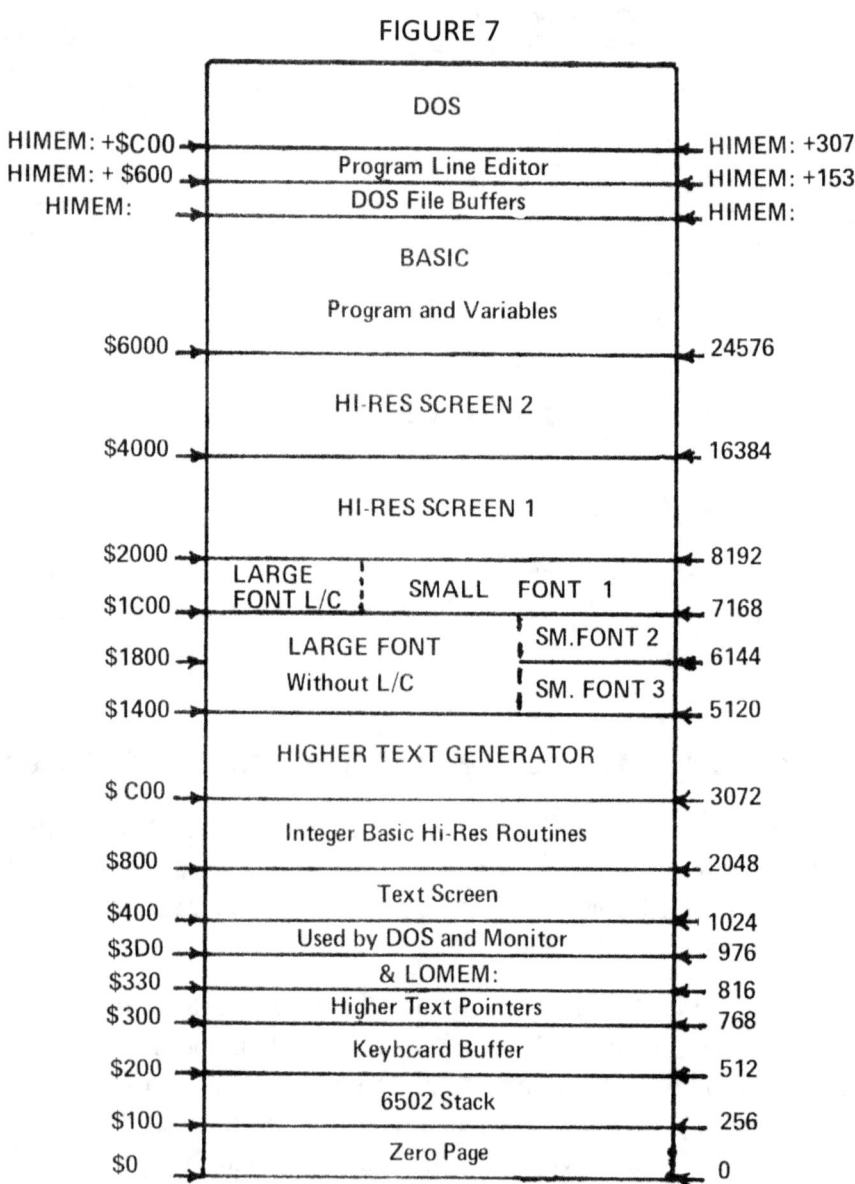

TABLE III

Hex	Dec	Label	Comments
302	770	COLOR	Current color number
303	771	FONT2	Large font pointer
304	772	FONT1	Regular font pointer
305	773	CTPTRL	
306	774	CTPTRH	
307	775	BKGNDL	
308	776	BKGNDH	
309	777	YSAV2	
30A	778	LWRFLG	
30B	779	LRFLG1	
30C	780	SIZFLG	
30D	781	INVFL2	
30E	782	SCLFLG	
30F	783	CLKFLG	Key click flag
310	784	MSKFLG	
311	785	BLDFLG	
312	786	BSTFLG	
313	787	CSTFLG	
314	788	EXPAN1	
315	789	EXPAN2	

3. High Resolution Screen Pointers

It is possible to draw on the hi-res screen page not currently in use, while continuing to view the present screen, by changing the value of the hi-res screen pointer. These pointers are located as follows: $E6 [230] for Applesoft, $326 [806] for Integer BASIC. A $20 [32] will permit drawing on Page 1; a $40 [64] will permit drawing on Page 2, thus, from Applesoft, POKE 230,64 would allow you to draw on Page 2 while continuing to view Page 1.

B. Font Configurations

1. Normal Configurations

The normal area for font storage is from $1400 [5120] to
$1FFF [8191]. There are three possible font configurations, as
shown in Figure 2, page 25. The default font, the one loaded in with
Higher Text, contains one large font without lower case, and one
complete small font. It is referenced in Figure 2 as "Configuration 'A'
(standard)".

One complete small font will occupy the same amount of
memory as the lower case portion of a large font; three complete small
fonts will take up the same memory space as a complete large font,
thus it may be seen that in "Configuration 'B'", we have three small
fonts which store in RAM at $1400 [5120], $1800 [6144], and $1C00
[7168] , respectively. No specific action is required on your part to
determine which configuration is saved to disk as a font or generator;
this is established solely by the present data in memory.

Saving a font from either editor will result in saving all memory
from $1400 [5120] to $1FFF [8191], unless small font 1, 2 or 3 is
specified in the save parameters, in which case only the appropriate
$400 [1024] of memory will be saved. If a generator is specified,
memory will be saved starting at $7FD [2045].

2. Non-Standard Configurations

There may be times when you wish to have available more than
one font configuration at a time, for example, a large font of standard
characters, and a large font of Old English or another contrasting style.
A *Higher Text* font may be loaded into any area of memory where
space is available. The table below shows where the index registers
are located, and the values to assign to them. In addition, in Applesoft,
it will be necessary to use the &LOMEM: utility to protect the area
used by the special font allocation. Use of &LOMEM: is explained on
page 45.

3. Calculating Font Indexes

The Index to the starting address of the large font is held in decimal location 771; the small font starting address index is held in 772 decimal. The index values may be changed with a POKE, either in immediate mode or from within the program, thus it is possible to change fonts "on the fly." To calculate the index for a large font, divide the starting address by 256, and subtract 4. The result may be POKEd into 771. A small font starting address should be divided by 256 (no subtraction required) and POKEd into 772.

Suppose you wished to use a second large font starting at $4000 [16384]. You would then add the following statements to the beginning of an Applesoft program:

```
200   PRINT D$"BRUN LOMEM:"
210   &LOMEM:19456: REM 16384 + 3072
  .
  .
500   POKE 771,60: REM(16384/256) -4
```

To the extent that free memory allows, you may have as many fonts in memory at one time as you wish. To determine the starting address of the next font to be specially located, add the length of the last font loaded to the starting address, using the following lengths:

Font Type	Length
One small font	$400 [10.24]
One large font (complete) or one large upper case and one small font	$C00 [3072]
One large font, no lower case	$800 [2048]

TABLE IV
Selected Font Indexes

Font Type	Address	POKE	Index
small	$1400 (5120)	772	20
large	$1400 (5120)	771	16
small	$1800 (6144)	772	24
small	$1C00 (7168)	772	28
small	$4000 (16384)	772	64
large	$4000 (16384)	771	60
large	$6000 (24576)	771	92

4. "Garbage" Fonts

When the font configuration calls for a mixture of a large font without lower case and one small font, small fonts nos. 2 and 3 will appear on the edit screen as garbage, seemingly random collections of lines and hash marks, etc. In reality, what is being viewed is the upper case of the large font. Conversely, while in the large font editor under the same circumstances, the lower case will display as unintelligible garbage.

C. Integer BASIC Hi-Res Routines

Despite the fact that Hi-Res graphics commands are not built into the Apple II Integer BASIC, a convenient scheme for referencing the subroutines and their parameters by name has been devised, as illustrated below:

Traditional Method	Improved Method
POKE 800,X MOD 256	X0 = X
POKE 801,X > 256	
POKE 802,Y	Y0 = Y
POKE 812,C	COLOR = C

The first statement (after BRUNing the Higher Text generator) of a program using the Hi-Res Subroutines should be:

```
1  X0= Y0= COLOR =SHAPE= ROT= SCALE
```

The purpose of this statement is to enter the first six BASIC variable names in the symbol table in a fixed sequence. When executed, each of the six parameters will be assigned storage at fixed locations relative to the address contained in the BASIC "start of variables" pointer, LOMEM, making them readily accessible by the Hi-Res routines.

The following statement lists all of the new Hi-Res subroutine entry initializations available to BASIC programs. These routines operate similar to the ones described in the old *Apple II Reference Manual*:

```
5  INIT=2048 : CLEAR= 2062 : BKGND =2865 :
   POSN = 2809; PLOT= 2830 : LINE = 2836 :
   DRAW = 2871 : DRAW1 = 2874: XDRAW = 2884 :
   XDRAW1 = 2887 :
   FIND = 2556
```

The allowable color specification values may also be referenced by name, if the initialization statement below is included in your program. Note that "GREEN" is preceded by "LET" to avoid a syntax error due to confusion with the "GR" command:

```
8  BLACK= 0: LET GREEN= 42: VIOLET= 85: WHITE=
   127: ORANGE= 170: BLUE= 213: BLACK2 = 128:
   WHITE2 = 255
```

For further information on these routines consult the *Higher Graphics* manual or the *Programmer's Aid #1* manual.

D. CTRL-B(ackground) Screen Functions

The common usage of Control-B is with the suffix 0, which sets the background color, as explained in Background Colors on page 16. The Control-B function is a highly technical achievement, complex and difficult for the first time user to comprehend. It extends the capabilities of *Higher Text* far beyond that of any other character generator currently available. A complete description of its various combinations and applications would require a manual unto itself, thus we will limit our coverage to conveying a general understanding of how it works, and its use for some applications.

Table V will give you an idea, in technical terms, of the operations performed. In 0-3 and 4-7 sequence, these are: EOR (exclusive OR) with the current color, OR the current page location, AND the page location, and EOR the page location. EOR, OR, and AND are Boolean operators which operate on binary data in a manner similar to the conventional add or subtract operators. A Boolean truth table is shown as Table VI. and in addition, you may be interested in getting a book from your library which more fully explains Boolean logic.

Table II on page 15 shows some 64 possible combinations of Font display mode/character color/background color using only Control B0. With some of the other Control-B suffixes, and using various color combinations on the second hi-res screen, literally hundreds of combinations are possible.

The Applesoft program listed on page 41 is a demo that will take you through these myriad combinations, nine at a time, and allow you to select the ones that are most appropriate for a particular application. A smooth scroll command (Ctrl-P) is imbedded in the program to give you time to see each variation before it scrolls away. Each sequence of nine possible character colors is interrupted with a request to "HIT ANY KEY" before proceeding. The current background mode and current character display mode are always in view at the top of the screen. A background of the six standard Apple hi-res colors in vertical bands is provided so that all possible combinations of font display modes and character colors may be viewed on each of the six backgrounds.

Note line 70: the DATA statement requires trailing spaces with each display mode name to fill out a total of nine characters.

The Ctrl-B(ackground) command performs two types of logical operations with the current character color, using one of the following as a reference:

a. the current character color
b. the current page background color
c. the alternate page background color

Operation type 1 is performed at the cursor position only. Operation type 2 is performed from the cursor to the end of line, and is executed only when a clear to end of line (Ctrl-N) command is issued. A table of these functions appears below.

TABLE V

Ctrl-B Functions

Command Code	Logical Operation	Type 1 at cursor	Type 2 to end of line
Ctrl B0	EOR	a	a
Ctrl B1	OR	b	–
Ctrl B2	AND	b	–
Ctrl B3	EOR	b	–
Ctrl B4	EOR	a	c
Ctrl B5	OR	c	c
Ctrl B6	AND	c	c
Ctrl B7	EOR	c	c

The most common application of Control-B functions would be where you have an existing chart or graph you wish to label with text characters, and do not require a solid background. By BLOADing the chart to screen two and using the subroutines described below, you may create a composite screen of the chart and labels on screen one. A further enhancement of this might be to have charts on disk say for three different years and use the labeling program to place the same labels on each chart as it is displayed.

TABLE VI

Truth Table

AND

```
      0           0           1           1
and   0     and   1     and   0     and   1
      0           0           0           1
```

Used as a mask. If one input is zero, the result will always be zero. Used to clear any bit.

OR

```
     0          0          1          1
or   0     or   1     or   0     or   1
     0          1          1          1
```

If one operand is a one, the result will always be a one.

EOR

```
      0           0           1           1
eor   0     eor   1     eor   0     eor   1
      0           1           1           0
```

If any bit is different, the result will always be non-zero. The EOR of FF will always produce the complement. EOR is used for comparisons.

Another example could be more closely related to the multi-color demo background, where your own background is composed of two or more colors, and you find your characters do not display properly on all of the backgrounds. The demo program can show you alternate combinations of Control-C (character color) and Control-B (background function) that would solve the problem.

Subroutine 80 sets up access to the second hi-res page, line 20 clears the screen, line 30 draws the vertical color bars, and subroutine 90-95 returns to screen one and transfers the contents of screen two to screen one, so that the same background is now on both screens.

```
5    REM  HIGHER TEXT CHR/BG COLOR DEMO
10   PRINT CHR$ (4)"BRUN LOMEM :": & LOMEM: 24576
15   PRINT CHR$ (4)"BRUN HIGHER TEXT"
20   GOSUB 80: HCOLOR= 0: FOR I = 0 TO 20: HPLOT 0,I TO
     279,I: NEXT
30   FOR I = 0 TO 7: HCOLOR= I: FOR J = 20 TO 191:
     HPLOT 35 * I,J TO 35 * I + 34,J: NEXT J ,I: GOSUB
     90: PRINT CHR$ (16);
35   FOR BG = 0 TO 7 PRINT CHR$ (3);0; CHR$ (2);0;
     CHR$(18); CHR$ (25): VTAB 1 : PRINT "BACKGROUND
     MODE NBR : "BG;
40   FOR CHR = 1 TO 7: READ L,M,CH$ :PRINT CHR$ (L);
     CHR$ (M);
45   VTAB 1: HTAB 24: PRINT CHR$ (3);0; CHR$ (2);0;
     CHR$ (18); CHR$ (25)" CHR= " ; CH$; CHR$ (L); CHR$
     (M);: PRINT : POKE 34,2 : GOSUB 80 : GOSUB 90
50   IF BG > 3 THEN PRINT CHR$ (3);9; CHR$ (2);0; CHR$
     (12) : REM CLEAR PG 1 TO BLACK
55   VTAB 4 : FOR CLR = 0 TO 9: PRINT CHR$ (3);0; CHR$
     (2);0;CLR; CHR$ (3);CLR, CHR$ (2);BG;" THIS IS A
     TEST USING COLOR NBR  ";CLR; CHR$ (14): NEXT CLR:
     PRINT CHR$ (2);0; CHR$ (3);0
60   HTAB 11: PRINT "HIT ANY KEY";: CALL -756 :NEXT
     CHR: RESTORE: NEXT BG: PRINT: PRINT "DONE": CALL
     -1220 :END
70   DATA 18,26,REG      ,18,25,REG-BOLD ,20,26,TALL
     ,20,25,TALL-BOLD,26,17,LARGE   ,23,23 ,WIDE
     ,5,5,EXPANDED
80   POKE 230,64: POKE -16304,0: POKE -16302,0: POKE
     -16297,0: POKE -16299,0: RETURN
90   POKE 230,32: POKE -16300,0
95   PRINT CHR$ (2);7; CHR$ (12): RETURN: REM MOVE SCRN
     2 TO SCRN 1
```

Note the GOSUB 80: GOSUB 90 at the end of line 45. This serves as -16302,0 a "refresh" for screen one, since some of the background will be destroyed by each cycle of nine color tests. You may wish to note this in particular, as it could prove handy in a future program.

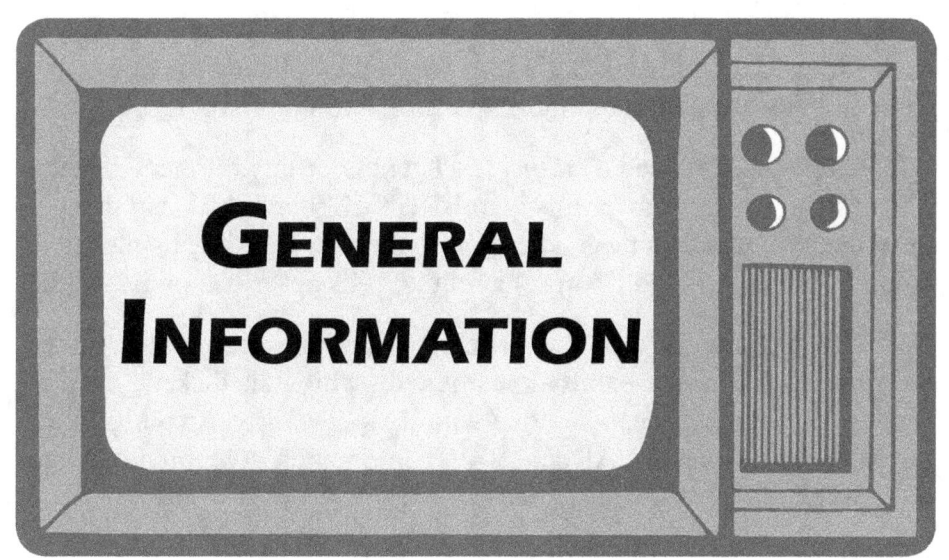

A. Creating Your Own Program Diskette

First you need to prepare a fresh diskette using the DOS INIT routine. You must determine whether your program is in Integer BASIC or Applesoft, then type INT or FP, whichever is appropriate to the program. Then, assuming you want the new diskette to boot and run your program, type INIT FILENAME, Vn, where FILENAME is the name of the program you will later save, and n is the volume number you wish DOS to assign to this diskette.

The disk drive will run for a minute or so, INITing the new diskette, and when it is finished, the flashing cursor will return. You have now initialized the disk and can load your programs, generator and fonts onto it. To perform said copy tasks, we recommend you use *Copy II Plus 8.5* or other similar disk file copy utility which will allow you to place your files on the disk. You can also SAVE and BSAVE files directly to the initialized disk.

If you plan to save an Applesoft program, you will need the &LOMEM: utility on the new diskette. You can transfer this by using

43

the *FID* program (if available) or by inserting the *Higher Text* diskette in the drive and typing BLOAD LOMEM:, then placing the new diskette in the drive and typing BSAVE LOMEM:, A816, L160.

You will also need a *Higher Text* generator on your new diskette. The easiest way to transfer this is to BRUN Higher Text, Load the generator, switch diskettes and save it to the new diskette, using the *Higher Text* L(oad) and O(utput) commands as described on page 25.

The last step is to save your Integer or Applesoft program on the new diskette, using the same file name with which the diskette was INITed. This transfer can be done with the *FID* utility, if you have it, or with conventional LOAD and SAVE commands, switching diskettes in between.

B. Subsidiary Functions

1. Key Click

For those Apple owners with a "silent" keyboard, *Higher Text* has a built in "key click" function which simulates the normal sound made when a key is depressed and touches the key stop. From direct mode it is selected and deselected with a Control-V, which acts as a toggle. Under program control it may be selected with a POKE 783,128, and deselected with POKE 783,0.

2. Control-G (bell)

As a minor embellishment, *Higher Text* has modified the "beep" sound of the Apple's bell to a more pleasant and realistic sounding tone. The bell can be placed in a PRINT statement with a Control-G, or in Applesoft, with a CHR$(7). For those interested, the modified bell uses a pulse width modulated square wave, modulated by a ramp; for those not so interested, it still sounds pretty neat.

C. SUPPORTING PROGRAMS

1. Program Line Editor

Program Line Editor (PLE) is a very useful utility program, not included on this diskette. It is available separately from your *Higher Text* distributor.

In addition to its editing capabilities, it is helpful to users of *Higher Text* by virtue of its capability to permit direct entry of lower case characters. *PLE* uses the same control commands for lower case as does *Higher Text*, i.e., Ctrl-A and Ctrl-S.

Higher Text will automatically disable *PLE* when called, i.e., with a CALL 3075 or BRUN HIGHER TEXT. However, *PLE* may be used for editing your current program if you exit *HIGHER TEXT* with a reset (or Ctrl-Reset). It is not necessary to remove *PLE* from memory.

With *PLE* in memory, it is then possible to enter program lines in lower case without having Higher Text up. At the same time, it may also be used for its editing capabilities.

2. LOMEM: (The &LOMEM: Utility)

Higher Text and its related routines use that area of memory where an Applesoft program is normally stored, thus a means must be provided to relocate the Applesoft program. LOMEM: is a separate binary program with that capability. In a *Higher Text* generator, this must be done before any variables are declared, since they would be overwritten by the memory move routine called by LOMEM:. Two steps are required: LOMEM: itself must be BRUN by your program, and &LOMEM: [locn] must be executed in the program (where [locn] equals in decimal, the new starting address for the Applesoft program). A program line to perform the above might look like this:

```
100  PRINT CHR$(4); "BRUN LOMEM:":&LOMEM: 16384
```

This would set the start of the Applesoft program past the first hi-res screen. &LOMEM: may be used more than once in a program, if needed, but only in an upward direction. If so, variables will be overwritten, but the program will be moved intact. Using &LOMEM: in a downward direction will destroy both variables and program. The proper way to reset the start of program to its normal [default] address is with the FP command. Once &LOMEM: has been executed, any subsequent Applesoft program will LOAD to the new address. The start of program address is unaffected by the NEW, CLEAR or regular LOMEM: commands.

3. Billboard

Billboard is a BASIC program containing two programs selectable from the Billboard menu, each of which is covered in the following sub-sections. *Slidemaker* is a utility which facilitates "labeling" a saved hi-res screen; *Climber* is a program to input, display and center lines of hi-res text.

a. Slidemaker

Slidemaker is a utility by Robert C. Clardy. It is included with the *Higher Text* diskette as an aid to labeling hi-res pictures, charts, etc. It may be selected from the *Billboard* menu.

After running *Slidemaker*, you will be asked if you wish to BLOAD a previously saved screen. This would normally be answered yes, as it is assumed you wish to label an existing screen. Be sure you have placed the diskette with the saved screen in the drive before proceeding.

Following your response to the preceding question, the *Slidemaker* command menu will be displayed. It is illustrated below in Figure 8. In each case possible, the commands are designed to simulate those of *Higher Text*. All commands are control characters, since regular characters are used to write to the screen. The four cursor controls, K (up), H (left), I (right), and J (down) offer complete freedom in placing characters anywhere on the screen.

A Ctrl-U, followed by a numeral in the range 0-9 will select a text color just as *Higher Text's* Ctrl-C does. Colors and display modes may easily be intermixed, and Ctrl-F may be used to load a different font, so that even fonts may be intermixed. The escape key will take you to and from the command menu at any time without disturbing the contents of the hi-res screen.

FIGURE 8

Slide Maker Ctrl Commands

```
Control-

     A = UPPER CASE        N = CLEAR/EOL
     B = ERASE             O = CLEAR/EOP
     C = ---               P = ---
     D = LOAD/SAVE         Q = LARGE FONT
     E = EXPANDED FONT     R = REGULAR
     F = FONT SELECT       S = LOWER CASE
     G = ---               T = TALL TEXT
     H = BACKSPACE         W = COLOR
     I = SPACE RIGHT       V = KEY CLICK
     J = LINE FEED         X = WIDE TEXT
     K MOVE UP             X = WIPE TEXT
     L HOME CURSOR         Y = SET BOLD
     M RETURN CTRL         Z = CLEAR BOLD


     PRESS ESC TO SEE INSTRUCTIONS

         K
     H + I      ==> CURSOR MOVEMENT
         J
```

b. Climber

Climber, by David Kampschafer, is a simple but handy program which allows you to input up to 26 lines of text, and save them to a file for later reloading. *Climber*, as its name implies, is a scrolling mechanism, using *Higher Text's* smooth scroll mode, to do a continuous scroll of the saved text with optional centering. In addition to the command menu, shown below as Figure 9, other menus to choose character colors, etc., may be selected from the main menu. For best results, characters should be limited to 20 or 40 characters per line, depending on the font selected.

FIGURE 9

The Climber Ctrl Commands

```
F = FONT SELECT     U = COLOR
I = NEW TEXT        D = LOAD/SAVE
A = AUTO CENTER     X = EXIT
ESC = MENU

    PRESS RETURN TO BEGIN
```

4. Higher Fonts & Font Previews

Higher Fonts is a collective name applied to diskettes containing fonts that can be used with *Higher Text*. *Higher Fonts* can save you hours of valuable time by supplying ready made fonts for inclusion in your *Higher Text* programs.

There are three types of fonts: Small (.SF), Medium (.MF), and Large (.LF). Most Small fonts occupy only the top left position of the font editor, except for "GK", "Math" and "Small Fonts" that occupy two or three panels with more characters.

Next are samples of the wide variety of fonts available for use with *Higher Text Plus*. Over 90 fonts from *Higher Text*, *Higher Fonts*, and *Font Album* by Andrew Wicker of Wickerware Software are included on the disk images:

SMALL .SF

Apl

```
··‾‾<≤=≥>≠v–→,×.∕
0123456789+⊢¦÷:⊂
α⍳∩⌊ε_∇⍋∘¦∘'⎕⌷⊤∘
*?⍴⌈~↓⍵⊃↑⊆<      )∧
ABCDEFGHIJKLMNO
PQRSTUVWXYZ[  ] ▨
```

ASCII

```
!"#$%&'()*+,-./
0123456789:;<=>?
@ABCDEFGHIJKLMNO
PQRSTUVWXYZ[\]^_
'abcdefghijklmno
pqrstuvwxyz{|}~▨
```

ASCII2

```
■!"#$%&'()*+,-./
0123456789:;<=>?
@ABCDEFGHIJKLMNO
PQRSTUVWXYZ[\]^_
`abcdefghijklmno
pqrstuvwxyz{|}~■
```

Bar

```
■!"#$%&'()*+,-./
0123456789:;<=>?
@ABCDEFGHIJKLMNO
PQRSTUVWXYZ[\]^_
`abcdefghijklmno
pqrstuvwxyz{|}~▨
```

SMALL .SF

Block

```
 !"#$%&'[ ]*+,-./
0123456789:;<=>?
@ABCDEFGHIJKLMNO
PQRSTUVWXYZ[\]^_
'abcdefghijklmno
pqrstuvwxyz{|}~
```

Broadwy

```
 !"#$%&'()*+,-./
0123456789:;<=>?
@ABCDEFGHIJKLMNO
PQRSTUVWXYZ[\]^_
`abcdefghijklmno
pqrstuvwxyz{:}~
```

Byte

```
 !"#$%&'()*+,-./
0123456789:;<=>?
@ABCDEFGHIJKLMNO
PQRSTUVWXYZ[\]^_
`abcdefghijklmno
pqrstuvwxyz{|}~
```

Color1

```
 !"#$%&'()*+,-./
0123456789:;<=>?
@ABCDEFGHIJKLMNO
PQRSTUVWXYZ[\]^_
`abcdefghijklmno
pqrstuvwxyz{|}~
```

SMALL .SF

Color2

Digital

Educational

Enhanced

SMALL .SF

Even

■ ! " # £ % & ' ( ) ✱ + , — . /
0 1 2 3 4 5 6 7 8 9 : ; < = > ?
@ A B C D E F G H I J K L M N O
P Q R S T U V W X Y Z [\ ] ^ _
` a b c d e f g h i j k l m n o
p q r s t u v w x y z { | } ~ ▦

Fancy

■ ! " # $ % & ' ( ) ✱ + , — . /
0 1 2 3 4 5 6 7 8 9 : ; < = > ?
@ A B C D E F G H I J K L M N O
P Q R S T U V W X Y Z [\ ] ^ _
` a b c d e f g h i j k l m n o
p q r s t u v w x y z { | } ~ ▓

Games

  ! " # $ % & ' [ ] ✱ + , — . /
0 1 2 3 4 5 6 7 8 9 : ; < = > ?
@ A B C D E F G H I J K L M N O
P Q R S T U V W X Y Z [\ ] ^ _

GK1

  ° | | ⎯ ⎯ = C € ✱ ± , — . /
0 1 2 3 4 5 6 7 8 9 . / < ≠ > ∞
→ α β Γ Δ δ φ ψ Π I J K Λ M N Ω
Π Q Ρ Σ Θ Υ Ω X ( ) | \ ] ^ _
` a b c δ η ₀ 1 2 3 4 5 6 7 8 9
ψ q r σ τ u v ω x y ς Γ |] ~ ●

52

SMALL .SF

GK: 1

2

Gothic

Graphics

SMALL .SF

Greek

Hebrew

Height

Large

54

SMALL .SF

Math: 1

2

3

Ninety

SMALL .SF

Normal

```
      ! " # $ % & ' ( ) * + , - . /
    0 1 2 3 4 5 6 7 8 9 : ; < = > ?
    @ A B C D E F G H I J K L M N O
    P Q R S T U V W X Y Z [ \ ] ^ _
    ` a b c d e f g h i j k l m n o
    p q r s t u v w x y z { | } ~
```

Outline

```
      ! " # $ % & ' ( ) * + , - . /
    0 1 2 3 4 5 6 7 8 9 : ; < = > ?
    @ A B C D E F G H I J K L M N O
    P Q R S T U V W X Y Z [ \ ] ^ _
    ` a b c d e f g h i j k l m n o
    p q r s t u v w x y z { | } ~
```

Pinball

Rune

```
      ! " # $ % & ' ( ) * + , - . /
    0 1 2 3 4 5 6 7 8 9 : ; < = > ?
    @ A B C D E F G H I J K L M N O
    P Q R S T U V W X Y Z [ \ ] ^ _
    ` a b c d e f g h i j k l m n o
    p q r s t u v w x y z { | } ~
```

SMALL .SF

Russian

```
   ! , # $ % & ' ( ) * + , - . /
 0 1 2 3 4 5 6 7 8 9 : ; < = > ?
 @ А Б В Г Д Е Ж З И Й К Л М Н О
 П Р С Т У Ф Х Ц Ч Ш Щ [ \ ] ↑ _
 ' а б в г д е ж з и й к л м н о
 п р с т у ф х ц ч ш щ ( | ) ~ ▓
```

Skinny

```
   ! " # $ % & ' ( ) * + , - . /
 0 1 2 3 4 5 6 7 8 9 : ; < = > ?
 @ A B C D E F G H I J K L M N O
 P Q R S T U V W X Y Z [ \ ] ↑ _
 ' a b c d e f g h i j k l m n o
 p q r s t u v w x y z ( | ) ~ ▓
```

Slant

```
   ! " # $ % & ' ( ) * + , - . /
 0 1 2 3 4 5 6 7 8 9 : ; < = > ?
 @ A B C D E F G H I J K L M N O
 P Q R S T U V W X Y Z [ \ ] ↑ _
 ' a b c d e f g h i j k l m n o
 p q r s t u v w x y z ( | ) ~ ▓
```

Slant2

```
 ■ ! " # $ % & ' ( ) * + , - . /
 0 1 2 3 4 5 6 7 8 9 : ; < = > ?
 @ A B C D E F G H I J K L M N O
 P Q R S T U V W X Y Z [ \ ] ^ _
 ' a b c d e f g h i j k l m n o
 p q r s t u v w x y z ( | ) ~ ▓
```

SMALL .SF

Small Fonts: 1

```
 !"#$%&'()*+,-./
0123456789:;<=>?
@ABCDEFGHIJKLMNO
PQRSTUVWXYZ[\]↑_
`abcdefghijklmno
pqrstuvwxyz(|)~▓
```

2

```
 !"#$%&'()*+,-./
0123456789:;<=>?
@ABCDEFGHIJKLMNO
PQRSTUVWXYZ[\]^_
`abcdefghijklmno
pqrstuvwxyz(|)~■
```

3

```
 !"#$%&'()*+,-./
0123456789:;<=>?
@ABCDEFGHIJKLMNO
PQRSTUVWXYZ[\]↑_
`abcdefghijklmno
pqrstuvwxyz(|)~▓
```

Special

```
■!"#$%&'()*+,-./
0123456789:;<=>?
@ABCDEFGHIJKLMNO
PQRSTUVWXYZ[\]^_
`abcdefghijklmno
pqrstuvwxyz(|)~■
```

SMALL .SF

Stencil

■ ! " # $ % & ' ( ) * + , - . /
0 1 2 3 4 5 6 7 8 9 : ; < = > ?
@ A B C D E F G H I J K L M N O
P Q R S T U V W X Y Z [\ ] ^ _
` a b c d e f g h i j k l m n o
p q r s t u v w x y z { | } ~ ▮▮

Stop

! " # $ % & ' ( ) * + , - . /
0 1 2 3 4 5 6 7 8 9 : ; « = » ?
@ A B C D E F G H I J K L M N O
P Q R S T U V W X Y Z [\ ] ^
` a b c d e f g h i j k l m n o
p q r s t u v w x y z ‖ # # ▦

Thin

■ ! " # $ % & ' ( ) * + , - . /
0 1 2 3 4 5 6 7 8 9 : ; < = > ?
@ A B C D E F G H I J K L M N O
P Q R S T U V W X Y Z [\ ] ^ _
` a b c d e f g h i j k l m n o
p q r s t u v w x y z { | } ~ ▯

Western

■ ! " # $ % & ' ( ) * + , - . /
0 1 2 3 4 5 6 7 8 9 : ; < = > ?
@ A B C D E F G H I J K L M N O
P Q R S T U V W X Y Z [\ ] ^ _
` a b c d e f g h i j k l m n o
p q r s t u v w x y z { | } ~ ■

59

SMALL .SF

White

Wicker

MEDIUM .MF

ASCII

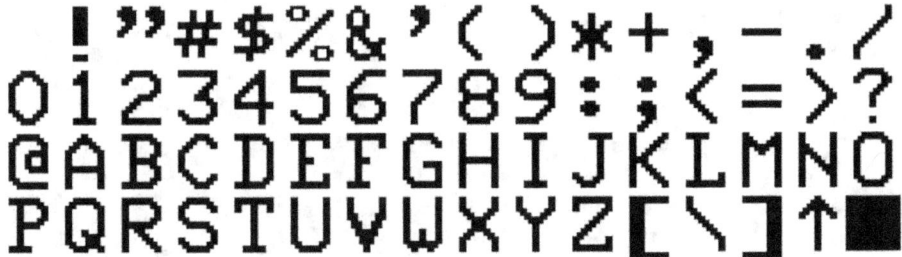

Backgrounds

Broadway

MEDIUM .MF

Hebrew 2

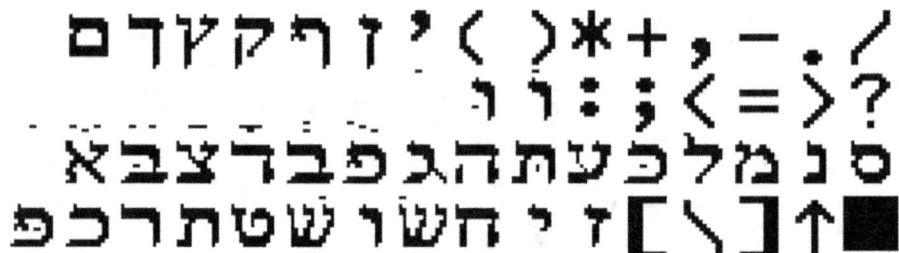

Quote

Raised

MEDIUM .MF

Runes

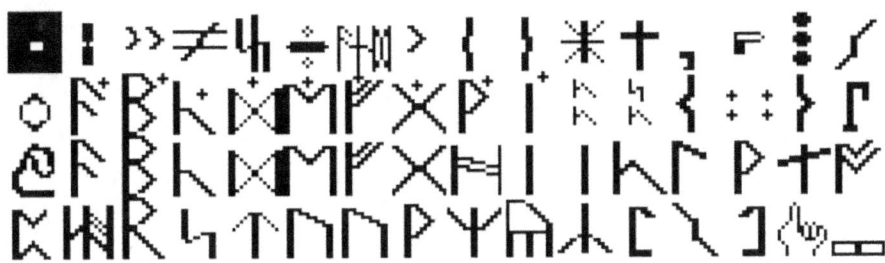

Shaded

Shadow

LARGE .LF

Apple

```
  ! " # $ % & ' ( ) * + , - . /
0 1 2 3 4 5 6 7 8 9 : ; < = > ?
@ A B C D E F G H I J K L M N O
P Q R S T U V W X Y Z [ \ ] ↑ _
  ' a b c d e f g h i j k l m n o
p q r s t u v w x y z { | } ~ 
```

Arabic

```
  !  "  "  "  !
+  :  :    ٩ ٨ ٧ ٦ ٥ ٤ ٣ ٢ ١
                        
_                          † 
                          ~ 
```

65

LARGE .LF

ASCII

Aust

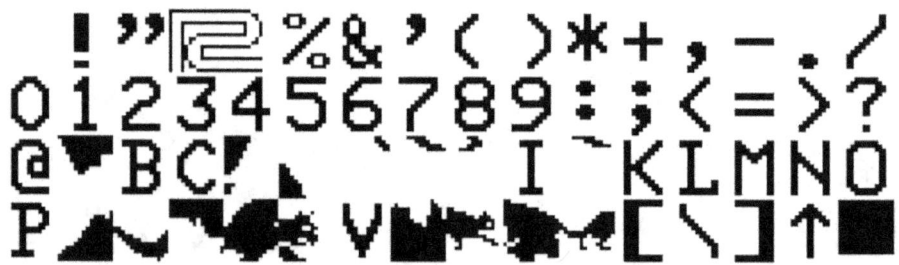

LARGE .LF

Balloon

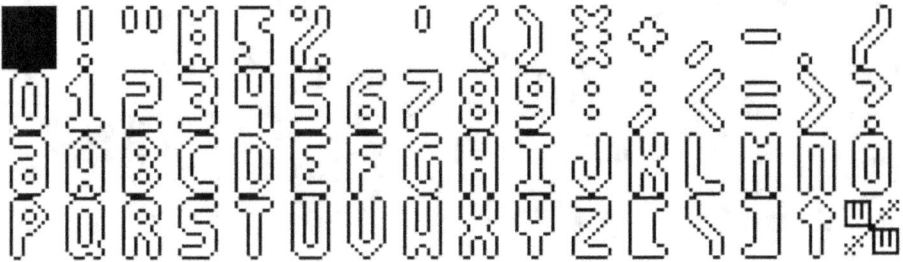

Block

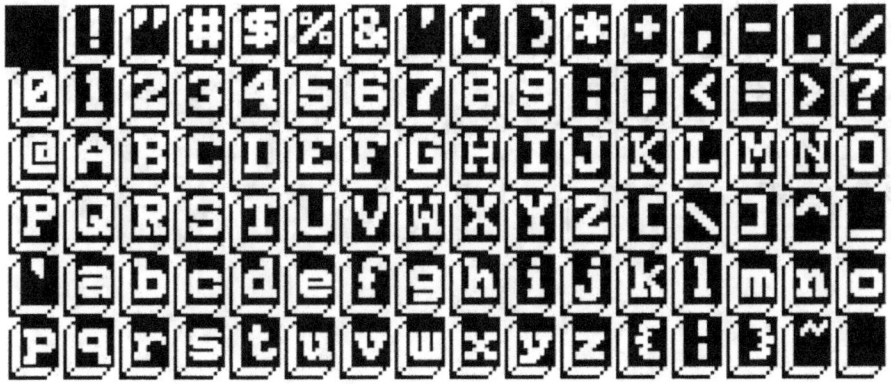

LARGE .LF

Block2

Broadway

LARGE .LF

Building

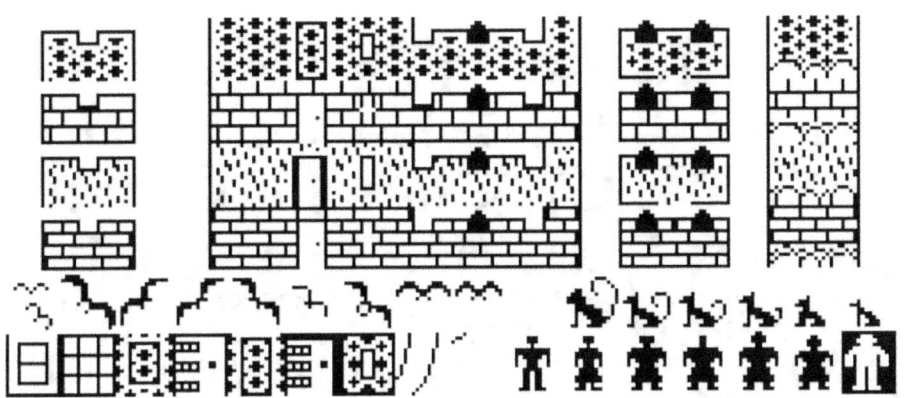

Carved

LARGE .LF

Celtic

! "⧉$⧉⧉ ' ⧉⧉ * + , - . /
0 1 2 3 4 5 6 7 8 9 : ; < = > ?
ɑꞅꞓꝺⱸꝼᵹhıjkℓɱɴo
pqꞅꞃꞅꞇuvⱳxᵹȝ[\]↑
⧉ɑꞃꝺⱸꝼᵹh ⧉⧉ ꝺɱɴ⧉
⧉⧉ꞃⱳ⧉ ⧉⧉⧉ y ⧉⧉ ■

Charleston

■ ! " # $ % & ' ( ) * + , - . /
0 1 2 3 4 5 6 7 8 9 : ; < = > ?
@ A B C D E F G H I J K L M N O
P Q R S T U V W X Y Z [\ ] ↑ _
' a b c d e f g h i j k l m n o
p q r s t u v w x y z { | } ~
...

LARGE .LF

Connect

Countdown

LARGE .LF

Educational

Egyptian 1

LARGE .LF

Egyptian 2

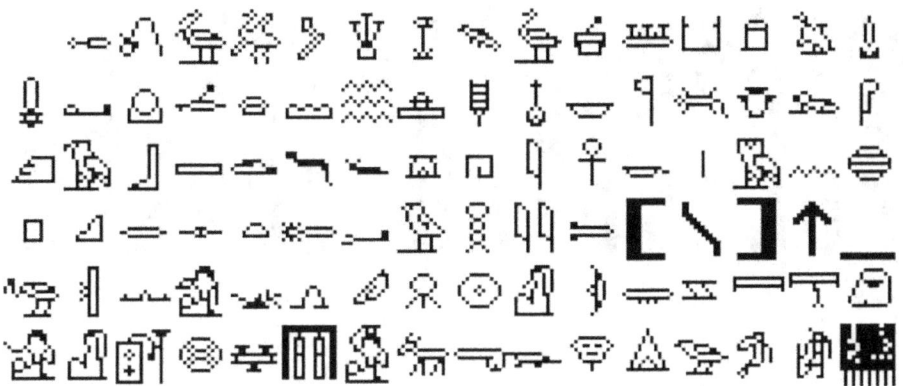

Expanded

!"#$%&'( )*+,-./
0123456789:;<=>?
@ABCDEFGHIJKLMNO
PQRSTUVWXYZ[\]↑_
`abcdefghijklmno
pqrstuvwxyz{|}~▨

LARGE .LF

Filled

Games

LARGE .LF

Grey

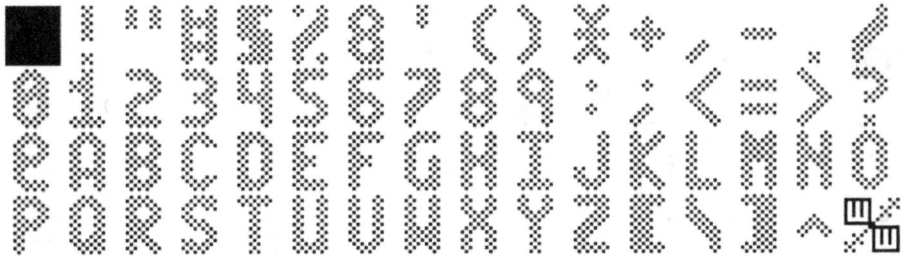

Hebrew 1

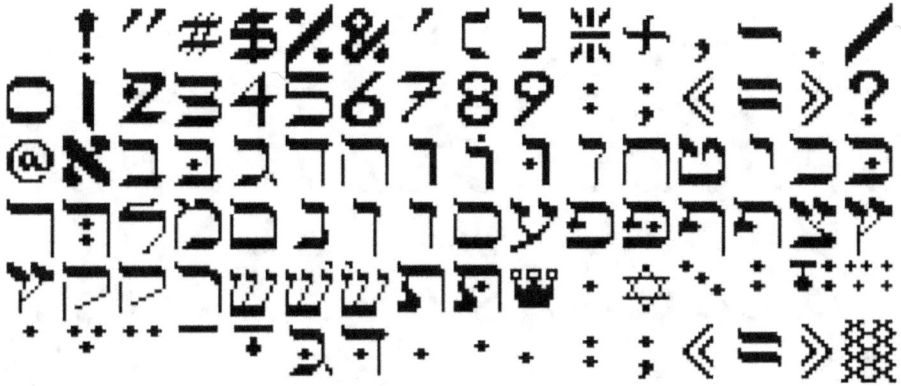

LARGE .LF

IBM

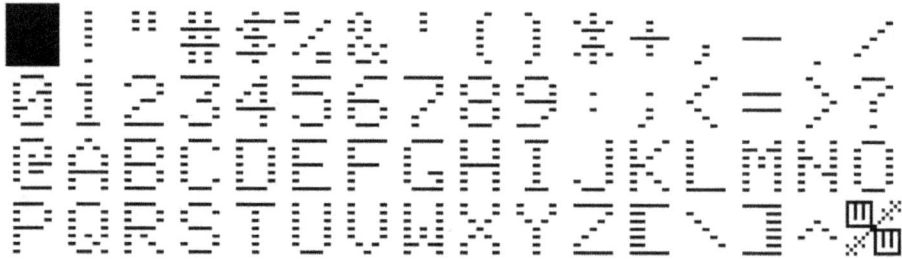

Italics

LARGE .LF

LitApl

```
     ! " # $ % &  ' ( ) * + , - . /
0 1 2 3 4 5 6 7 8 9 : ; < = > ?
@ A B C D E F G H I J K L M N O
P Q R S T U V W X Y Z [ \ ] ↑ _
  ' a b c d e f g h i j k l m n o
p q r s t u v w x y z { | } ~
```

Ninety

LARGE .LF

Normandia Italic

! ” # $ % & ’ ( ) * + , – . /
0 1 2 3 4 5 6 7 8 9 : ; < = > ?
@ A B C D E F G H I J K L M N O
P Q R S T U V W X Y Z [\ ] ↑ _
‘ a b c d e f g h i j k l m n o
p q r s t u v w x y z { ¦ } ~ ▨

Old English

! ” £ $ 4 & ’ ( ) * + , – . /
0 1 2 3 4 5 6 7 8 9 : ; < = > ?
@ A B C D E F G H I J K L M N O
P Q R S T U V W X Y Z [\ ] ↑ _
‘ a b c d e f g h i j k l m n o
p q r s t u v w x y z { ¦ } ~ ▨

LARGE .LF

Oriental

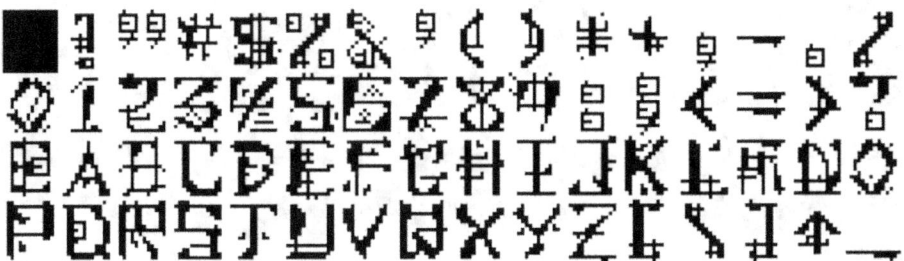

Outline

LARGE .LF

Pac

Pinball

LARGE .LF

Precise

Punic

LARGE .LF

Roman

! ” # $ % & ’ ( ) * + , — . /
0 1 2 3 4 5 6 7 8 9 : ; < = > ?
@ A B C D E F G H I J K L M N O
P Q R S T U V W X Y Z [\ ] ↑ _
‘ a b c d e f g h i j k l m n o
p q r s t u v w x y z { ¦ } ~ ▧

Round

82

LARGE .LF

Shadow

Space Font

LARGE .LF

Stencil

Stix

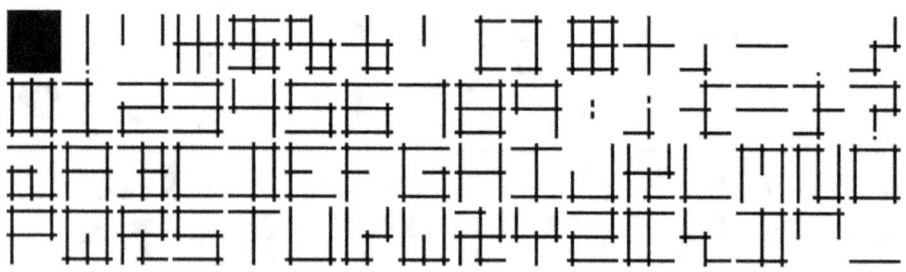

LARGE .LF

Three-D

...

Uncials

LARGE .LF

Wicker

---

5. Demo Programs

Back in the Overview, we made mention of the problems encountered when trying to LIST a *Higher Text* program with imbedded control characters. There is a fairly easy way to overcome this, and that is by setting up a standard set of subroutines to establish each usable control code as a subroutine, thus when the program is LISTed, the interpreter sees only the GOSUB, rather than a code that would cause it to change display modes in the middle of a LIST.

There are also other advantages to this method: because mnemonic names can be attached to the subroutines, there is never any doubt as to their function. The same routines can be used in many programs, and an EXEC file can be written so they may be EXECed into any new or existing program.

Listings of Applesoft and Integer BASIC subroutines follow: an EXEC file creator which may be used by either language also appears. In each listing, control characters are indicated by a "normal" character enclosed in square brackets. The square brackets should not be entered; just type the control character specified by typing the Ctrl key and the character key at the same time.

Applesoft Subroutines for *Higher Text*

```
10   REM   APPLESOFT SUBROUTINES FOR HIGHER TEXT

800  REG$ = CHR$ (18): WIDE$ = CHR$ (23): TALL$ = CHR$
     (20):EX$ = CHR$ (5): LRGE$ = CHR$ (12): BOLD$ =
     CHR$ (25): UNBOLD$ = CHR$ (26)
810  BG$ = CHR$ (2): B0$ = BG$ + "0": B1$ = BG$ +
     "1":B2$ = BG$ + "2": B3$ = BG$ + "3": B4$ = BG$ +
     "4": B5$ = BG$ + "5": B6$ = BG$ + "6": B7$ = BG$
     + "7"
820  CLR$ = CHR$ (3): WHITE$ = CLR$ + "0": GEEN$ =
     CLR$ + "1": VIOLT$ = CLR$ + "2": ORANGE$ = CLR$
     + "3": BLUE$ = CLR$ + "4": YELLOW$ = CLR$ + "5":
     LAVNDER$= CLR$ + "6": PINK$ = CLR$ + "?": AQUA$=
```

```
        CLR$ + "8": BK$ = CLR$ + "9"
830  HOM$ = CHR$ (12): ELN$ = CHR$ (14): EPG$ = CHR$
     (15): SCROLL$ = CHR$ (6): SMOOTH$ = CHR$ (16):
     QUITSMOOTH$ = CHR$ (0): RETURN: REM

900  PRINT REG$;: RETURN
901  PRINT WIDE$;: RETURN
902  PRINT TALL$;: RETURN
903  PRINT EX$;: RETURN
904  PRINT LRGE$;: RETURN
905  PRINT BOLD$;: RETURN
906  PRINT UNBOLD$;: RETURN

910  PRINT B0$;: RETURN
911  PRINT B1$;: RETURN
912  PRINT B2$;: RETURN
913  PRINT B3$;: RETURN
914  PRINT B4$;: RETURN
915  PRINT B5$;: RETURN
916  PRINT B6$;: RETURN
917  PRINT B7$;: RETURN REM

920  PRINT WHITE$;: RETURN
921  PRINT GEEN$;: RETURN
922  PRINT VIOLT$;: RETURN
923  PRINT OURANGE$;: RETURN
924  PRINT BLUE$;: RETURN
925  PRINT YELLOW$;: RETURN
926  PRINT LAVNDER$;: RETURN
927  PRINT PINK$;: RETURN
928  PRINT AQUA$;: RETURN
929  PRINT BK$;: RETURN REM

930  PRINT HOM$;: RETURN
931  PRINT ELN$;: RETURN
932  PRINT EPG$;: RETURN : REM

940  PRINT SCROLL$;: RETURN
941  PRINT SMOOTH$;: RETURN
942  PRINT QUITSMOOTH$;: RETURN
```

Applesoft *Higher Text* Demo

```
10 REM

APPLESOFT HIGHER TEXT DEMO
USE WITH FP SUBROUTINES

50 IF PEEK(2045)=76 THEN 90
60 PRINT CHR$(4);"BRUN LOMEM:" & LOMEM: 16384
70 PRINT CHR$(4);"BRUN HIGHER TEXT"
80 CALL 3072
90 GOSUB 800
300 FLAG=1:PRINT "DSP MODE (R/W/T/E/L) ": GET FT$
310 PRINT "BG COL (W/G/V/OBK) ": GET COL$
320 PRINT "CHR COL (W/G/V/O/B/Y/L/P/A/K) ": GET CH$
330 IF FT$="R" OR FT$="T" THEN PRINT "REG OR BOLD ":
    GET B$
400 ON FT$="R" GOSUB 900: ON FT4="W" GOSUB 902:: ON
    FT$ = "E" GOSUB 903::::: ON FT$ = "L" GOSUB 904
410 ON COL$ = "W" GOSUB 920: ON COL$ = "G" GOSUB 921:
    ON COL$ = "V" GOSUB 922:  ON COL$ = "O" GOSUB
    923: ON COL$ = "B" GOSUB 924: ON COL$ = "Y" GOSUB
    925: ON COL$ = "L" GOSUB 926: ON COL$ = "P" GOSUB
    927: ON COL$ = "A" GOSUB 928: ON COL$ = "K" GOSUB
    929
430 ON BS = "R" GOSUB 906: ON B$ = "B" GOSUB 905
440 IF FLAG THEN FLAG = 0: COL$= CH$: GOSUB 910: GOTO
    410
450 PRINT "HELLO": END
```

Integer BASIC Subroutines for *Higher Text*

```
10   REM  INTEGER BASIC SUBROUTINES  FOR HIGHER TEXT

100  REG=900: WIDE= 901: TALL= 902: EXPND = 903:
     LARGE=904: BOLD=905: UNBOLD=906
110  BKGND0=910: BKGND1=911: BKGND2= 912: BKGND3=913:
     BKGND4=914: BKGND5=915: BKGND6=916: BKGND7=917
```

```
120   WHITE=920: GREEN=921: VIOLET= 922: ORANGE=923:
      BLUE=924: YELLOW=925: LAVENDER=926: PINK=927:
      AQUA=928: BLACK=929
130   HOME=930: EOL=931: EOP=932: SCROLLUP=940:
      SMOOTH=941: UNSMOOTH=942


900   PRINT "[R]";: RETURN
901   PRINT "[W]";: RETURN
902   PRINT "[T]";: RETURN
903   PRINT "[E]";: RETURN
904   PRINT "[G]";: RETURN
905   PRINT "[Y]";: RETURN
906   PRINT "[Z]";: RETURN: REM

910   PRINT "[B]0";: RETURN
911   PRINT "[B]1";: RETURN
912   PRINT "[B]2";: RETURN
913   PRINT "[B]3";: RETURN
914   PRINT "[B]4";: RETURN
915   PRINT "[B]5";: RETURN
916   PRINT "[B]6";: RETURN
917   PRINT "[B]7";: RETURN: REM

920   PRINT "[C]0";: RETURN
921   PRINT "[C]1";: RETURN
922   PRINT "[C]2";: RETURN
923   PRINT "[C]3";: RETURN
924   PRINT "[C]4";: RETURN
925   PRINT "[C]5";: RETURN
926   PRINT "[C]6";: RETURN
927   PRINT "[C]7";: RETURN
928   PRINT "[C]8";: RETURN
929   PRINT "[C]9";: RETURN: REM

930   PRINT "[L]";: RETURN
931   PRINT "[N]";: RETURN
932   PRINT "[O]";: RETURN: REM

940   PRINT "[F]";: RETURN
941   PRINT "[P]";: RETURN
942   PRINT "[@]";: RETURN: REM
```

Integer BASIC *Higher Text* Demo

```
10   REM   INTEGER BASIC HIGHER TEXT DEMO
          USE WITH INTEGER SUBROUTINES

70   IF PEEK (2045)<>76 THEN PRINT "BRUN HIGHER TEXT" :
     REM CTRL D IN QUOTES
80   CALL 3072

300  FLAG=1: PRINT "DSP MODE (R/W/T/E/L) " : GOSUB
     600: FT: KEY
310  PRINT "BG COL (W/G/V/O/B/K) ": GOSUB 600: COL=KEY
320  PRINT "CHR COL (W/G/V/O/B/Y/L/P/A/K) ": GOSUB
     600: CH=KEY
330  IF FT= ASC("R") OR FT= ASC("T") THEN GOSUB 500
400  FT=((FT=210) +2 * (FT=215) +3 * (FT=212) +4 *
     (FT=197) +5 * (FT=204)+899): GOSUB FT
410  XX=(COL=215) +2 * (COL=199) +3 * (COL=214) + 4
     * (COL=207) +5 * (COL=194) +6 * (COL=217) +7 *
     (COL=204) +8 * (COL=208)
412  COL=XX + (9 * (COL=193) + 10 * (COL=203)+919):
     GOSUB COL
430  IF NOT FLAG THEN 450
440  FLAG=0: COL=CH: GOSUB 910: GOTO 410
450  PRINT "HELLO": END
500  PRINT "REG OR BOLD ": GOSUB 600: B= KEY: B=(B=
     194) +2 * (B= 210)+904: GOSUB B: RETURN
600  KEY= PEEK <-16384>: IF KEY < 128 THEN 600: POKE
     -16368,0: RETURN
```

EXEC File Create

```
10    REM   EXEC FILE CREATE

20    D$ = "": REM CTRL D
30    PRINT D$;"OPEN SUBFILE"
40    PRINT D$;"WRITE SUBFILE"
50    POKE 33,33
60    LIST 100,942
70    PRINT D$;"CLOSE"
80    TEXT: END
```

GLOSSARY

Definitions used in this glossary may often refer to terminology within the context of, or pertaining only to the characteristics of, the *Higher Text* program, and not necessarily to general usage.

ACCESS – To locate and retrieve data.

ADDRESS – Memory location, usually expressed in hex.

ALGORITHM – A sequence of steps which may be performed by a program or other process, which will produce a given result.

ALLOCATE – To set aside or reserve space.

ALPHABETIC CHARACTER – Any one of the letters A through Z (uppercase and lowercase).

ALPHANUMERIC – Consisting of letters, numbers, and other symbols such as punctuation marks and mathematical symbols.

APPLE – (1) The round fleshy fruit of a Rosaceous tree (Pyrus Malus). (2) A brand of personal computer. (3) Apple Computer, Inc. manufacturer of home computers.

APPLESOFT BASIC – A floating-point BASIC interpreter that is included in ROM. It was the successor to Integer BASIC. See *BASIC*.

ARGUMENT – The value on which a function operates.

ARITHMETIC OPERATOR – An operator, such as +, that combines numeric values to produce a numeric result.

ARRAY – Matrix of variable data. This data is accessed by programs to fulfill a need for table style data in an easy to manage format.

ASCII (American Standard Code for Information Interchange) – A character encoding standard that translates uppercase and lowercase letters and symbolic characters into a 7-bit binary representation having the values 0 to 127. The eighth bit, parity and framing bits are not part of this definition.

ASSEMBLER – A program used to translate as assembly language program into the machine language used by a processor.

ASSEMBLY LANGUAGE – A language similar in structure to machine language, but made up of "mnemonics" and "symbols" that are converted to the machine language of a processor by the assembler. Well-written assembly language programs usually run faster and use less memory than BASIC programs, but they usually take longer to write and longer to test and debug than BASIC programs.

BACKGROUND – In *Higher Text*, the field upon which characters are printed, also used as a color reference by the Ctrl-B function.

BASE – In number systems, the exponent at which the number system repeats itself; the number of symbols required by that number system.

BASIC (Beginner's All-purpose Symbolic Instruction Code) – A programming language that is designed to be easy to learn and use, and encourage people to use computers for simple problem-solving operations. Originally developed at Dartmouth College.

BINARY – The base 2 number system, composed solely of the numbers 0 and 1.

BINARY FILES – Binary files save machine language programs, binary data (which might be automatically gathered from sensors and generated by analog-to-digital converters), etc. Such material may be of arbitrary length and may include in its body any possible binary combination of bits.

BIT – Abbreviation for "Binary DigIT." Either of the binary digits 0 or 1. See *Byte*.

BLOAD – Binary program load.

BLOCK – Storage methodology used by ProDOS for placing data on a floppy disk. Under ProDOS, a 140K 5.25" floppy disk holds 280 blocks (0~279) of 512 bytes each.

BOOT – The process of starting a computer system ("booting up"). A cold boot is starting the computer after it was off. The operating system (DOS 3.3 or ProDOS) is loaded into memory. A warm boot is a reloading of the operating system without a power-down sequence.

BRANCH – To resume program execution at a new location. GOTO and JMP (jump) are branch instructions.

BRUN – Binary program run. The BRUN command in DOS 3.3 and ProDOS causes a binary program to be loaded into memory and run.

BSAVE – Binary program save. The BSAVE command in DOS 3.3 and ProDOS causes the binary data in some portion of memory to be saved as a disk file.

BUFFER – Large temporary memory storage area.

BUG – A program error, often called "an undocumented feature."

BYTE – The amount of storage required to represent one character. Hexadecimal or Decimal representation of eight binary bits: 0~255 in Decimal, $00~$FF in Hexidecimal. 8 bits = 1 byte. 1,024 bytes = 1K or Kilobyte.

CALL – Executes a machine language subroutine contained within the called memory location and onward. Continues until the program code contains an RTS.

CARRIAGE RETURN – The key used as an end of line or end of input terminator. Also called the RETURN key.

CATALOG – A list of all files stored on a disk, sometimes called a "directory."

CHARACTER – A single byte, letter, digit, or other symbol.

CHIP – Tiny pieces of silicon or germanium containing many integrated circuits that perform specific tasks for a computer.

CHR$(x) – Applesoft function which prints the alphanumeric or special character specified by the ASCII value assigned to x.

CLEAR – In the *Higher Text* editor, removes a dot from the matrix.

CODE – (1) A number or symbol used to represent some piece of information in a compact or easily processed form. (2) The statements or instructions that make up a program.

COMMAND – An instruction to the program, usually input by the user.

COMPILER – A program which translates a high-level language into the machine code used by a computer.

COMPLEMENT – In colors, the opposite; the color 180° opposed in a color wheel. Blue and orange are complementary colors.

CONCATENATE – To join together, making one character string from two, as in C$ = A$ + B$.

CONDITIONAL BRANCH – A branch that depends on the truth of a condition or the value of an expression.

CONFIGURATION – A specific group of software or hardware in a standard format.

CONSTANT – A symbol in a program representing a fixed, unchanging value. Compare to "Variable."

CONTROL CHARACTER – A special character created by simultaneously typing the "Control" key and another alpha character. These keys are used in the editor for cursor movement, text formatting, and other specified functions. Control-G can be shown as ^G.

CPU – Central Processing Unit. See *Microprocessor*.

CTRL – The "Control" key.

CURSOR – (1) A marker or symbol that delineates where the next action will take place. (2) A programmer who can't find the reason a program is crashing.

DASH (-) – Command that runs a BASIC, machine, EXEC, or interpreter program in ProDOS only.

DATA – Facts or information used by or in a computer program.

DEBUGGING – The process of detecting and correcting errors in a computer program.

DECIMAL – The base 10 number system, composed of the numbers 0 through 9, inclusive.

DECREMENT – Decrease value in calculated steps.

DEFAULT – Nominal value or condition assigned to a parameter when not otherwise specified by the user.

DELETE – Command that removes a file from its directory.

DELIMITER – Symbol to separate data fields.

DIRECTORY – List of files on diskette or part of a group of files on a hard drive. In ProDOS, each directory has a name rather than the "Slot x, Drive x, Volume x" designation in DOS 3.3.

DISKETTE – A 5.25" or 3.5" disk. Apple II 5.25" floppy disks typically hold 140K, and 3.5" disks typically hold 800K of data.

DISPLAY – The output of the Apple II or program to a television set or monitor.

DITHERING – A process of dot mixing to produce additional hi-res colors.

DOS – Disk Operating System such as DOS 3.3 or ProDOS. The user interface between a computer and the applications program. An OS allows the user to execute programs and perform disk operations.

DOT MATRIX – A grid or graph of specific dimensions used for drawing a character by placement of certain dots.

DUMMY – Data with no significance, "GET A$" is a dummy if used just to halt a program.

EDITOR – Text-editing program that allows text to be entered into a data file and manipulated as desired.

ENTER – A means to obtain access to a program or subroutine from keyboard or direct mode.

ERROR MESSAGE – Message that notifies the user of an error or problem in the execution of a task or program.

EXEC File – A DOS text file which, when called by the EXEC command, reads data into Apple II memory as if it were entered from the keyboard.

EXECUTE – Perform an action specified by a program or computer operator.

EXIT – A means to return to BASIC or direct mode from within a program.

EXPRESSION – A formula in a program describing a calculation to be performed.

FAC – Floating Point Accumulator.

FID – A file transfer utility on the Apple DOS 3.3 master diskette.

FIELD – Contains data which would not normally subdivide.

FILE – Data that has been saved to a diskette, such as a BASIC program or a word processing document.

FILENAME – Name of a file that has been saved to diskette.

FIRMWARE – Those components of a computer system consisting of programs stored permanently in read-only memory. Cards for printers and other devices contain firmware.

FLAG – A data bit used to indicate the state of a device or the result of an operation.

FONT – A specific *Higher Text* character set.

FORMAT – Prepare a blank diskette to receive and store information by dividing its surface into tracks and sectors.

FP (FLOATING POINT) – Floating Point BASIC as included in Applesoft.

GENERATOR – *Higher Text* operating system that includes at least one font.

HEX – Abbreviation of hexadecimal, the base 16 number system.

HEXADECIMAL – The base 16 number system, composed of the numbers 0 through 9, and A through F. Usually notated with a '$' prefix. Hexadecimal is a useful shorthand for describing the contents of a byte, with each hex digit describing half of a byte.

HEX DUMP – Formatted listing of hex data.

HIGH ORDER – The byte containing the value of the left most two digits of a hex expression.

HI-RES – High-Resolution graphics.

HOME – The normal or default position of a cursor.

IMBED – To implant or place within.

IMMEDIATE MODE – The normal condition of an Apple II when a program is not running and commands may be entered from the keyboard.

INCREMENT – Increase value in calculated steps.

INITIALIZE – (1) To set to an initial state or value in preparation for some computation. (2) To prepare a blank disk to receive information by dividing its surface into tracks and sectors.

INPUT – (1) Information transferred into a computer from an external source, such as a keyboard, disk drive, or modem. (2) The act or process of transferring such information.

INSERT – In editing, to place additional characters within a string or to add dots to a matrix.

INTEGER – Number without fractional parts in the range -32768 to +32767.

INTEGER BASIC – The BASIC interpreter for the first Apple II. Succeeded by Applesoft BASIC.

INTERPRETER – A program which translates instructions written in a high level to machine code as the program is executed.

INTERRUPT – (1) To temporarily stop a process. (2) A signal created by either hardware or software to demand the immediate attention of a machine's CPU, there by stopping execution of any code that is being executed by said CPU. (3) In data communications, to take an action at a receiving computer that causes the ending computer to end a transmission.

INVERSE – The opposite of, usually applying to the Inverse Mode in text fonts or numbers.

I/O (Input/Output) – The transfer of information in and out of a computer. Used frequently in connection with peripheral devices.

IRQ – Interrupt requests.

JUMP – Another term for a branch.

KILOBYTE (K or KB) – Used with numbers to denote "kilo" or one thousand. 1K = 1,024 bytes. 64K is 64 times 1,024 bytes, or 65,536 bytes.

LABEL – Symbolic name for an address, often expressed in mnemonic form.

LINE – One line of text on the display screen. In Text Mode, 23 lines are available.

LINEFEED – Moves the cursor on the screen down one line. The ASCII character is Control-J.

LOAD – Command that brings a BASIC program into memory from a file.

LOADER – Program that calls up machine code from mass storage and loads it into memory for execution.

LOCK – Command that protects a file from being accidentally renamed, deleted, or altered.

LOGICAL OPERATOR – An operator, such as AND, that combines logical values to produce a logical result.

LOOP – Section of a program that is executed repeatedly until some condition is met such as an index variable reaching a specified ending value.

LOW ORDER – The byte containing the value of the right most two digits of a hex expression.

LO-RES – Low-Resolution graphics.

L.S.B. – The Less Significant Byte of the two-byte pair.

LSB – Least Significant Bit.

MACHINE LANGUAGE – Data groups which are interpreted as instructions to be executed by the processor. See *Assembly Language*.

MEMORY – See *RAM (Random Access Memory)*.

MEMORY LOCATION – A unit of main memory that is identified by an address and can hold a single item of information of a fixed size. In the Apple II, a memory location holds one byte, or 8 bits of information.

MENU – A screen display allowing the user to select from a number of options.

MICROPROCESSOR – A computer processor contained in a single integrated circuit, such as the Apple II's 6502 or 65C02 microprocessor.

MNEMONIC – Symbolic abbreviation containing characters helpful in remember an application or function, such as an assembly language instruction.

MOD – Algorithm which returns the remainder of a division operation (must be simulated in Applesoft BASIC).

MODE – A particular sub-type of operation.

MODULE – A portion of a program devoted to a specific function.

MONITOR – (1) A closed-circuit television receiver. (2) A program which allows you to use your computer at a very low level, often with the values and addresses of individual memory locations. Monitor commands are used to communicate with the Monitor.

M.S.B. – The More Significant Byte of the two-byte pair.

MSB – Most Significant Bit.

NIBBLE (or Nybble) – (1) A 4-bit unit of data, or half a byte. (2) One of the best and longest-running magazines for the Apple II and Mac, created by entrepreneur and business expert Mike Harvey. (3) "What are we going to call this series of bits? How about a bite, but spell it with a 'y'! So what do we call half a byte? A 'nybble', obviously!" (attributed to Werner Buchholz at IBM, circa 1956.)

NULL – Having no value.

NUMERIC – An ASCII character in the 0-9 range.

OBJECT PROGRAM – The program produced by a compiler or interpreter from a high-level program.

OFFSET – Value, often used with or as an index to locate related data and add to a base value.

OPERATOR – A symbol or sequence of characters such as + or AND, specifying an operation to be performed on one or more values (the operands) to produce a result.

OUTPUT – (1) Information transferred from a computer to some external destination, such as the display screen, a disk drive, a printer, or a modem. (2) The act or process of transferring such information.

PAGE – Each page of memory in Apple II computers consist of 256 bytes. That is to say, $00 to $FF would be one page. A 32K machine would have 128 pages, a 48K machine would have 192 pages, while a 64K machine would contain 256 pages of memory. After the Zero Page ($0000~$00FF), each page is described by the first two digits of its 4 digit hexadecimal address.

PARALLEL – A method of data handling in which all the bits composing a word are transmitted simultaneously.

PARAMETER – A constant or value that a program requires to function, often specified by the user.

PARSER – Section of interpreter that formats listing of a BASIC program.

PATH – A specified route to a specific subdirectory used in ProDOS.

PC – Program Counter.

PEEK – BASIC command which returns the decimal value of a specified memory location.

PERIPHERAL – An external device connected to a computer such as a printer, modem, monitor, or disk drive.

POINTER – A register memory location containing the memory address of data or instructions.

POKE – BASIC command which stores a decimal value in a specified memory location.

PR# – Command that sends output to the Apple II slot number specified.

PREFIX – A settable pathname that indicates a directory file.

PROCESSOR – A generic term for that part of computer hardware performing arithmetic and logical operations. See *Microprocessor*.

ProDOS – The major operating system for Apple II computers, that stands for Professional Disk Operating System.

PROGRAM – A sequence of instructions to be followed by the computer to carry out desired operations.

PROGRAM CONTROL – Normally used to refer to instructions issued while a program is running.

PROMPT – To remind or signal the user that some action is expected, typically by displaying a distinctive symbol, a reminder message, or a menu of choices on the display screen.

PROTECT – To prevent an area of memory from being overwritten.

QUIT – Exiting a program and returning to the operating system.

RAM (Random Access Memory) – The volatile, temporary storage area in the computer that requires power to maintain its contents.

RAM DRIVE – The use of RAM to emulate a disk drive for temporary drive storage.

READ – To transfer information into the computer's memory from a source external to the computer (such as a disk drive or modem), or into the computers processor from a source external to the processor (such as a keyboard or main memory).

REGISTER – Single RAM memory or microprocessor storage location, usually for temporary use. A, X, Y-Registers and S, P, PC-Registers.

RELATIONAL OPERATOR – An operator, such as >, that compares numeric values to produce a logical result.

RENAME – Change the name of the file.

RESET – A key, which is part of a combination that causes the computer to re-boot a program. To Stop and warm start the computer.

RESIDES – A specific memory area in which a program or data may be found.

ROM (Read Only Memory) – A memory device from where operating instructions and other programs reside permanently and cannot be altered or added to.

ROUTINE – A program which performs a specified task or function.

RS-232 – A standard voltage interface allowing a serial connection between the computer's communications port and an external device such as a modem or a printer.

RUN – The command to execute a BASIC program.

RWTS – Read-Write Track-Sector. These are the Diskette input and output routines.

SAVE – Command to save the BASIC program currently in memory to a file on disk.

SCROLL – To move a line of text (usually upward) on the screen.

SECTOR – The tracks on Apple 5.25" diskettes are subdivided into sectors. The sector is the smallest unit of information that can be written to, or read from, a diskette at one time. Each sector contains one memory page (256 bytes) of usable information. Each track contains the same number of sectors, so the physical length inches or centimeters of a sector on the outermost track is longer than that of a sector on the innermost track. Sectors on the outermost track and the innermost track take the same amount of time to pass by the read head.

SERIAL – A method of data handling in which the bits composing a word are transmitted one after the other.

SET – In the *Higher Text* editor, to place a dot in the dot matrix.

SLAVE DISKETTE – A disk that has been formatted for a specific system type and will only boot on that system type.

STACK – A section of memory used to hold addresses or data items. The page of 256 memory locations from $0100 to $01FF (decimal 256~511) is called the Apple System Stack, as well as memory Page 1. The Stack is used in conjunction with the S-Register or Stack Pointer to provide positive control of the system in situations where control is passed from one portion of a program to another.

STATEMENT – An instruction line in a high-level language. In BASIC, smallest portion of a program complete in itself. Delimited by a ':' or end of line.

STRING – A group of ASCII characters that are alpha, numeric, punctuation, or control.

SUBROUTINE – A section of frequently used operations in a program which are treated as small separate programs.

SUFFIX – In *Higher Text*, a portion of a command that requires additional preceding data.

SYNTAX – The formal structure of an argument or command.

SYNTAX ERROR – An error which specifies to the user that the structure of the line of BASIC code is improperly formatted or that it is missing a required element such as quotation marks.

SYSTEM – A collection of routines or programs operating as a single entity or program.

TABLE – List of values, words, data, etc. that may be referenced by a program.

TEXT – A line or string of ASCII characters.

TEXT FILE – A file containing an arbitrary string of ASCII characters interspersed with occasional carriage returns to specify the end of a line.

TEXT SCREEN – The normal Apple II screen display, not used by *Higher Text* or other graphical programs.

TOGGLE – To switch from one mode to another. In *Higher Text*, this is usually performed by issuing the same command.

TOKEN – One byte hex representation of a BASIC or other high level language command.

TRACE – A debugging method in which the program is executed one instruction at a time, and sometimes the register contents can be examined after each step.

TRACK – Apple 5.25" diskettes have 35 tracks under DOS 3.3. Each consists of a circular recording path at a fixed distance from the center of the disk. Thus, each is like a very thin, at ring, concentric with all the others. They are numbered from 0 (the outermost track) to 34 (the innermost track).

VAL – Applesoft command that solves the value of a string. Also, the founder of A.P.P.L.E.

VARIABLE – Alphanumeric representation which may assume or be assigned a number of values.

VECTOR – Address to be branched to.

VOLUME – In DOS 3.3 and ProDOS, volume refers to floppy disk and hard drive storage.

VTOC (Volume Table of Contents) – On a 5.25" diskette Sector 0 of Track 17 (the track which is equidistant from the innermost and outermost tracks) is reserved for the VTOC.

WHY – Questions that programmers ask that have no answer.

WINDOW – Portion of screen display blocked off for special use.

WOZ – Steve Wozniak, an Apple Computer Inc. co-founder, inventor of the Apple-1 and Apple II computers, all-around genius, nice guy, über geek, philanthropist, and longtime supporter of the A.P.P.L.E. user group.

WRITE – To transfer information from the computer to a destination external to the computer (such as a disk drive or modem) or from the computers processor (such as main memory).

WWA – *What's Where in the Apple: Enhanced Edition* – a very useful programming reference book, also published by A.P.P.L.E.